ANDRÉ MALRAUX

MODERN LITERATURE MONOGRAPHS
GENERAL EDITOR: Lina Mainiero

In the same series:

S. Y. AGNON *Harold Fisch*
SHERWOOD ANDERSON *Welford Dunaway Taylor*
LEONID ANDREYEV *Josephine M. Newcombe*
ISAAC BABEL *R. W. Hallett*
SIMONE DE BEAUVOIR *Robert Cottrell*
SAUL BELLOW *Brigitte Scheer-Schäzler*
BERTOLT BRECHT *Willy Haas*
ALBERT CAMUS *Carol Petersen*
WILLA CATHER *Dorothy Tuck McFarland*
JOHN CHEEVER *Samuel T. Coale*
COLETTE *Robert Cottrell*
JOSEPH CONRAD *Martin Tucker*
JULIO CORTÁZAR *Evelyn Picon Garfield*
JOHN DOS PASSOS *George J. Becker*
THEODORE DREISER *James Lundquist*
FRIEDRICH DÜRRENMATT *Armin Arnold*
T. S. ELIOT *Joachim Seyppel*
WILLIAM FAULKNER *Joachim Seyppel*
FORD MADOX FORD *Sondra J. Stang*
JOHN FOWLES *Barry N. Olshen*
MAX FRISCH *Carol Petersen*
ROBERT FROST *Elaine Barry*
GABRIEL GARCÍA MÁRQUEZ *George R. McMurray*
MAKSIM GORKI *Gerhard Habermann*
GÜNTER GRASS *Kurt Lothar Tank*
PETER HANDKE *Nicholas Hern*
LILLIAN HELLMAN *Doris V. Falk*
ERNEST HEMINGWAY *Samuel Shaw*
HERMANN HESSE *Franz Baumer*
CHESTER HIMES *James Lundquist*
HUGO VON HOFMANNSTHAL *Lowell W. Bangerter*
UWE JOHNSON *Mark Boulby*
JAMES JOYCE *Armin Arnold*
FRANZ KAFKA *Franz Baumer*
SINCLAIR LEWIS *James Lundquist*
GEORG LUKÁCS *Ehrhard Bahr and Ruth Goldschmidt Kunzer*
NORMAN MAILER *Philip H. Bufithis*
ANDRÉ MALRAUX *James Robert Hewitt*
THOMAS MANN *Arnold Bauer*
CARSON MCCULLERS *Richard M. Cook*
ALBERTO MORAVIA *Jane E. Cottrell*
VLADIMIR NABOKOV *Donald E. Morton*
ANAIS NIN *Bettina L. Knapp*
FLANNERY O'CONNOR *Dorothy Tuck McFarland*
EUGENE O'NEILL *Horst Frenz*
(continued on page 150)

ANDRÉ MALRAUX

James Robert Hewitt

FREDERICK UNGAR PUBLISHING CO.
NEW YORK

For Peter and
our Paris then

Printed in the United States of America
Design by Anita Duncan

Library of Congress Cataloging in Publication Data

Hewitt, James Robert.
André Malraux.

(Modern literature monographs)
Bibliography: p.
Includes index.
1. Malraux, André, 1901–1976. 2. Authors, French—20th century—Biography.
PQ2625!A716Z6813 843′.9′12 [B] 70-15661
ISBN 0-8044-2379-2

Contents

Chronology

1901	3 November: Georges André Malraux is born in the Montmartre section of Paris
1905–18	Raised by his divorced mother and maternal grandmother in suburban Bondy
1919–20	Works for a bookseller; makes his débuts in Parisian literary circles
1921	Marries Clara Goldschmidt; trip to Italy
1923	Travels to Indochina with his wife; is arrested for "theft" of ancient Cambodian art treasures
1925	Publishes an anti-colonial newspaper in Saigon
1926	Returns to Paris and starts writing about his experiences in the east
1928	*Les Conquérants* is published, a critical and commercial success
1929–32	Extensive world travel with Clara; *La Voie royale*, a fictionalized account of his Indochina adventure, is published
1933	*La Condition humaine* is published; Malraux is awarded the Prix Goncourt for fiction
1934	Journeys to Moscow and Berlin; undertakes a flight over the Arabian desert, claiming to "discover" the lost kingdom of Sheba
1935	*Le Temps du mépris* is published
1936	Joins the republican side in the Spanish Civil War; sets up an international air squadron

1937	Goes to the United States in behalf of the Spanish republican cause; *L'Espoir* is published
1938	Returns to Spain to make a film based on *L'Espoir*
1940	World War II spreads; Malraux, an enlisted man in the tank corps, is captured, then escapes. In prison camp, begins a new novel.
1943	*Les Noyers de l'Altenburg* is published in Switzerland.
1943–45	Active in the French underground resistance, he adopts the pseudonym "Colonel Berger;" leads a brigade in Alsace-Lorraine in final days of war
1945–46	Serves briefly as De Gaulle's propaganda chief in the first post-war government
1948–50	Increasingly active in gaullist politics; champions the General's *Rassemblement du Peuple Français,* is accused of betraying liberalism
1951	*Les Voix du silence* is published to widespread acclaim and controversy
1952–57	Continues to write unorthodox studies on world art and civilization
1958	De Gaulle returns to political power; Malraux serves as Minister of Cultural Affairs for ten years
1965	After an illness, takes a world cruise; meets with Nehru and Mao as De Gaulle's "ambassador"; contemplates writing a book of recollections
1967	*Antimémoires* is published: acclaim and controversy
1968	Follows De Gaulle into political retirement
1971	*Les Chênes qu'on abat* is published, commemorating De Gaulle
1972	Confers with Richard M. Nixon prior to the President's trip to China; in November, suffers a near-fatal heart attack
1974	*La Tête d'obsidienne,* a tribute to Picasso, and *Lazare,* an account of his brush with death, are published

1975–76 Produces new volumes on art; revises his sequel to *Antimémoires*. 23 November 1976: Malraux dies of pulmonary congestion in Paris, shortly after his seventy-fifth birthday

1

A Dark Stranger

On a foggy night in the autumn of 1948, André Malraux stood on the podium of the Palais de la Mutualité, not far from the heart of the Latin Quarter, his coat loosely draped over his shoulders, a cigarette hanging from his lips. It was a scene of *déjà vu.* For two decades this prize-winning novelist, his stormy life a popular legend, had been a dominant and controversial figure in the literary and political worlds. On innumerable occasions, in this same auditorium and others throughout Paris, he had held the spotlight defending liberty and liberalism. Tonight he was speaking as the champion of General Charles De Gaulle and the newly formed Gaullist party, *Rassemblement du Peuple Français*: a "rallying" of the French people.

It was an audience of workers, bourgeois, intellectuals, students—some rabidly partisan, some there to listen and judge, some to disrupt. At mid-point in his speech, Malraux was interrupted by hecklers. With familiar theatricality, he moved forward from the rostrum, his coat still resembling a cape, that inevitable cigarette bobbing up and down as he launched out at them: "We waited for you communists for weeks and months on end in Spain; you will wait now until I finish speaking!"

There could be no doubt in the minds of most listeners, whether for or against Malraux, for or against De

Gaulle, Malraux was dramatizing here the fact that in 1936, while he and his fellow combatants, Spanish Loyalists and their sympathizers from all over the world, had been doing daily battle against Franco's fascist forces, the Russians, who were supposedly Loyalist allies, repeatedly kept failing to send the promised aid that might have helped assure victory. And in this bitterly anti-communist accusation lay the crux of the controversy surrounding Malraux in 1948. He was accepted throughout France and the world as one of the great novelists of his time. In *La Condition Humaine* (Man's Fate), he had passionately recorded the struggles of the Chinese in their revolution of the 1920s, and in *L'Espoir* (Man's Hope), a novel of the Spanish Civil War, he had poeticized the "lyric illusion" of a people struggling to keep Spain free; in his short 1935 novel, *Le Temps du Mépris* (Days of Wrath), he had taken a fiercely anti-fascist stand against Nazism, warning the world of the terror to follow. Everything about his life and work seemed to establish him as unequivocally liberal.

He was even thought to be not just left wing, but either communist, pro-communist, a sympathizer or "fellow traveler." Now allied with General Charles De Gaulle (thought to be right-wing, reactionary, totalitarian, perhaps fascist), Malraux appeared a political paradox. Was he not a traitor to the libertarian ideas he had expressed as a novelist? So asked the left, while De Gaulle's supporters, largely on the right, wondered: could Malraux be trusted? To be sure, he had fought valiantly in the French underground Resistance during World War II—but then the Resistance had boasted many communists!

At forty-seven, Malraux had lived the most flamboyantly adventurous of lives, frequently in the news either for his writings or his daredevil exploits and participation in major world events. He had recently abandoned fiction and produced a book on art and civilization that proved as controversial as his association with De Gaulle. A man of many colors and careers, he had served briefly as the General's Minister of Information in 1945 and was now at his side again in a new crusade for power.

What baffled most observers, and infuriated many, were Malraux's relentless attacks on communism; for a European intellectual with liberal credentials, his haranguing against Russia sounded for all the world like a diehard conservative of the American midwest. To understand Malraux's apparent "defection from the Left," and his unabashed admiration for De Gaulle, requires a thorough exploration of his works, the progression of his thought from the 1920s forward. As a preface to that analysis, it is useful first to examine the climate of 1948 and the cause that Malraux was supporting.

Once a mighty power, an empire of sorts, France found herself war-torn and weak. The people, while hoping for hope, saw the future as uncertain. Freed from the Nazi occupation, breathing a certain fresh air of national pride again, most Frenchmen felt nonetheless torn between the giant powers, the United States and Russia. Fearing a new outbreak of war, they felt compelled to choose sides, and so the nation was split, and also splintered by its many political parties, with few French really believing in France.

What De Gaulle sought, and in some ways symbolized himself, was a revitalized French unity based on past—and future—glory. He *dared* the people to choose France. Proposing a break with historical colonialism, he envisioned the former French colonies throughout the world as voluntary members of a great French "union." Not particularly pro-American, De Gaulle preached an independent France as spiritual leader of a new Europe, but saw the menace to his reunification program in the monster to the East: Stalinism. André Malraux, a life-long partisan of human justice, shared not only the General's policy of liberation but his dream of a "paternalistic" empire. From internationalist he had become nationalist, a champion of traditional French virtues and values—but also a new kind of internationalist, a partisan of the new Gallic union. And like De Gaulle, but for other reasons too as we shall see, a rabid anti-communist, much to the confusion and disappointment of many of his admirers.

Beyond the political paradox of Malraux, however, there was the enigma of the Malraux "legend." Although books and articles had been published about him, and he would freely give interviews about his own works and ideas, Malraux spoke little of his personal life, and little was known. Though none claimed to have all the facts or could vouch for their accuracy, biographers and critics had constructed a makeshift sketch of Malraux's life which Malraux himself rigorously refused to confirm or contradict. As of 1948, sounding altogether like a fictional adventure, it was generally believed that he had gone to Indochina as a young man on an archeological mission (perhaps governmental?), gotten into trouble of sorts, then served as liaison officer with Shanghai revolutionaries in the 1920s, flown a mysterious mission over Arabia in the '30s, commanded an air squadron in Spain, and fought with the French Resistance. What was *certain*, however, was that he had written widely acclaimed novels, incorporating bold philosophical ideas within powerful tales of adventure, and that these tales appeared to be based on experience, reflecting aspects of the extraordinary Malraux legend. From the start, fact mingled with fiction.

Since 1948, new biographical light has been shed, and a good deal of the myth has been doubted or discredited. But yet another turn occurred. When, at age sixty-six, André Malraux set about publishing a series of recollections (not memoirs or autobiography, he stoutly insisted), their brilliant interplay of fact, fancy, and occasional outright fiction, showed Malraux to be basically a man fascinated by greatness and a great "fascinator" himself, one of the most fascinating figures of our time: an activist novelist of international reputation, knowledgeable in politics, art, history, and philosophy, war and death, weapons and words, who had seemed at one point to be the "man of the twentieth century."

Georges-André Malraux was born on 3 November 1901, an only child. His father came from Dunkirk, the Flemish seaport; his mother, from the Jura mountain region near Switzerland, although her ancestry was Italian. During the three years their marriage lasted, the couple lived in the Montmartre quarter of Paris, but André's childhood was spent for the most part in the small gray suburb of Bondy where he was raised by his divorced mother and maternal grandmother. Eager to explore the wonders of Paris and in need of adult male companionship, the boy looked forward to Sundays and holidays with his father. These ended when the older Malraux went off to war in 1914.

For a man who is now regarded as one of the giant intellects of the century, André Malraux's formal education was limited and undistinguished. Only a modest scholar from the start, he managed to pass the rigorous examinations for entrance to the Lycée Condorcet, one of the finest in Paris. He soon disappeared from the classroom, however, and while still in his teens, persuaded his mother and grandmother to advance sufficient funds for him to set up a Paris apartment of his own.

Physically, Malraux was always slight of build, wiry if not athletic, quick in his movements and in his walk. Although he continued to convey an appearance of lean vigor throughout most of his life, he seems to have severely reproached the inevitable paunchiness that comes with age. In a close-up photograph taken in the 1960s, Malraux is wearing a leather jacket whose creases are clearly accentuated. Referring to the coat rather than his face, Malraux wryly quipped: "Too many wrinkles." The nervous tics, the twitching of face and hands, so pronounced in Malraux's frequent television appearances as elder statesman and philosopher during the 1970s, were not signs of age, however, but were already manifest when he was still a young man.

The pose that young Malraux cultivated was that of a dilettante of the arts—not the languorous hothouse variety of esthete popular in turn-of-the-century life and lore but rather a new breed of *active* amateur-connoisseur. Ever on the move, frequenting libraries, book shops and book stalls, art shops, galleries and museums, he rapidly acquired a vast store of knowledge embracing virtually an entire world history of art and literature. Or so it seemed. Speaking of medieval poetry, African or Hindu art, he would rattle on at such speed, and with an authority approaching dogmatism, that his captive listeners could not tell whether this startling, enthusiastic youth was genius or charlatan.

Malraux's most distinguishing natural feature was always his eyes: dark, birdlike, hypnotic, holding his audience, whether one or many, as prisoner or prey. His slick black hair developed its own eccentricity, and Malraux early acquired yet another "tic:" brushing back the unruly lock that persistently fell forward again over his forehead. The gesture seemed to say: "I will not be tamed." Another characteristic of Malraux's "tough guy" defiance was the inevitable cigarette, either dangling from a corner of his mouth or on which he seemed to be drawing, deep in solitary thought. There was always about André Malraux that Byronic quality the French call *un beau ténébreux*: a dark stranger.

Clearly not destined for any conventional career, Malraux attached himself to a bookseller specializing in rare and de luxe editions. At his leisure, whether randomly or with the intuition of the connoisseur, he would scour likely sources and turn up almost daily with sought-after texts or with an unusual "find" that was sure to prove marketable. Instinctively adept in the world of letters, Malraux soon made his début as an editor, overseeing the publication of a variety of books ranging from a devout *Passion de Jésus-Christ* to works by the Marquis de Sade and other underground erotica.

With no formal training, he seemed to have a natural talent for designing books of elegant format and typography. Frequenting artists as well as writers, he showed fine perception in selecting the illustrations for the books he edited. Soon he was writing prefaces as well, and also publishing articles on a myriad of subjects: cubist art, cubist poetry, writers as diverse as moralist André Gide and pre-surrealist poet Lautréamont. He was altogether immersed in the feverish artistic activity that had burst forth in Paris just after world war I.

There was nothing "bohemian" about Malraux, however; he was always impeccably tailored, given to pinstripe suits and silk ties. There was almost something of the dandy about him. He liked to dine in the best restaurants, and although his income cannot have been that great, he would make a great show of paying the bill for a party of his friends. Among them, oddly enough, was Max Jacob, a veritable prototype of the bohemian poet, who shared a room with the young Spanish painter Pablo Picasso.

Jacob was Malraux's opposite in every respect. He was short and unattractive, with baggy clothes that gave him the look of a clown. Malraux was all seriousness and erudition. He would monologue endlessly on writers and writings, painters and painting; no style, no era seemed alien to him. His rush of words and dogmatic tone gave the impression that he was knowledgeable in primitive or christian art, the medieval epic and the romantic lyric.

Max was all caprice and fantasy, with a great gift for mimicry. He would leap up from the table, improvise a poem, a song, a dance, and leave his audience helpless with laughter at his mockery, which was often self-mockery. Born a Jew, but later to become a Catholic recluse, Max Jacob had the gentle complexity of a saint—the clown who would play Hamlet. He was also homosexual, and took the curious but dead-serious Malraux to Le Boeuf sur le Toit and other bars in Paris where men wearing make-up danced together and the bartender might do a spontaneous strip-tease. In later years, Jacob took to spoofing his ertswhile companion, calling him "wise old Malraux" and wondering if he would not end up as a stuffy university professor. Meanwhile, the nineteen-year-old Malraux paid the tribute of dedicating his first published fiction to Max Jacob. It was called *Lunes en Papier* (Paper Moons)—and worthy of Max's *fantaisie* it was!

In this short fantastic tale, teeth fall out of the moon, turn many colors, change from musical notes into paper flowers, and are finally transformed into balloons being sold by a stuffed toy cat. It is a wonderland of cartoon-like graphics, a festival of imagery rendered in bizarre, almost surrealist, poetic prose—a far cry from the style Malraux would later forge, writing of revolution in China and war in Spain. In yet another metamorphosis, the "paper moons" emerge as allegorical Deadly Sins, and set out to kill Death.

A funny old man called God has changed his name to Satan, and although nobody, including God, notices the difference, Satan now rules the world with Death as his chief deputy. Death is a woman wearing a smoking jacket that covers her aluminium rib cage. She is tricked into taking a corrosive acid bath, and after a few last sensuous puffs on her cigarette, expires. In ironic conclusion, the Deadly Sins cannot seem to remember why they wanted to kill Death in the first place.

The book, under Malraux's supervision, was superbly printed, with illustrations by Fernand Léger, and created a momentary stir in the Paris cafés frequented by writers and artists, then was quickly forgotten. *Lunes en papier*, however, is more than a juvenile curiosity. For all the differences in stylistics, one finds there key elements that will mark Malraux's more serious work: nihilism, agnosticism, irony, and a fascination with death. It is evident that the author of *Lunes en papier* sees a world in chaos but also in metamorphosis, and metamorphosis will be one of Malraux's guiding philosophical and esthetic premises. There is also the fundamental question: can man conquer death, or is this an idle pursuit?

In *Lunes en papier*, Malraux calls the kingdom of death the kingdom of "*Farfelu*"—an archaic medieval-renaissance word he resurrected and which came to be identified with him, finding its way back into French dictionaries when Malraux reached the height of his fame. *Farfelu* is a word so rich in mulitple meanings that it virtually defies translation.

It means wild, crazy, wacky, zany, far-flung, and also far-fetched. That which is "*farfelu*" is not only in the realm of the strange and improbable, it partakes of the grotesque and the bizarre. There is a connotation of *scary*, in the sense of those "fun houses" or "haunted houses" one used to find in amusement parks. Malraux's *royaume-farfelu* is thus a kingdom of death with Hallowe'en trappings. By extension, he who dares brave the *farfelu* is himself a boldly reckless and foolhardy *farfelu* adventurer. If there were a single English word to sum up Malraux's complex meaning, it might be "daredevil." But there was little about his life to date that would suggest that quality.

In June, 1921, at a luncheon of writers and artists, Malraux met Clara Goldschmidt, who can best be described in contemporary terms as "liberated." A Jew of German origin, she was more intellectual and more spirited than any girl he had known or imagined. Essentially a misogynist, as Clara would later point out, Malraux for the moment had met his female match. Since both families were against their marrying, the couple ran off to Italy where Malraux, who had never been there, gave Clara whirlwind tours of the great museums, with running commentary. Back in Paris, they won approval for a later October wedding, just a few days before Malraux's twentieth birthday.

Although he was working sporadically as an art book editor, and continued to contribute articles to literary magazines, Malraux was not established professionally. Dipping into Clara's dowry, they were able to indulge their taste for travel: to Belgium, Germany, and Greece. They were fascinated by all that was new in the young twentieth century: experimentation in the arts, airplane travel, the movies. They would sit up half the night discussing the new painters and poets, the films of Charlie Chaplin, and German expressionist films like *The Cabinet of Doctor Caligari.* But Malraux's *farfelu* spirit craved more expansion and more adventure than even Europe of the 1920s could provide.

2

Keys to the Kingdom

Those who had read or even heard about Malraux's playfully surrealistic *Lunes en Papier* had good reason to be surprised by its contrast in tone and style with the tragic density of his first two novels. *Les Conquérants* (The Conquerors), published in 1928, deals with very real events, those of the drama-charged summer of 1925 when revolution in China was erupting, destined to change the future of millions and the face of the globe in modern times. *La Voie Royale* (The Royal Way), in 1930, recounts a more personal adventure. It is the story of two men invading the jungle of Cambodia in search of a ruined temple known for its Indochinese art treasures. This, too, is based on a certain reality; although cast in the form of fiction, it parallels an actual adventure undertaken by Malraux several years earlier.

It was with the publication of these two novels that the Malraux "legend" took shape. Both literary critics and general readers were aware that the author had spent time in the east, and it came to be assumed that both *La Voie Royale* and *Les Conquérants* were rooted in direct personal experience and first-hand observation. Throughout his entire life, Malraux remained scrupulously reticent about discussing his personal life and activities. Thus, in the absence of documentation, and since he made no effort to contradict the growing legend, two beliefs were widely, if erroneously, held. Up until the 1950s, biographers generally accepted that Malraux had headed an official government archeological expedition to Indochina, and that he had then served in some advisory capacity with the Kuomintang (Chinese Nationalist Party).

We now know, however, that while Malraux had indeed been to Indochina, he had not yet set foot in Canton or Shanghai, nor in any way played an active role in the Chinese revolution of which he wrote. With regard to the Cambodian experience, this is a splendid example of transforming, or confusing, fact and fiction. Far from leading an official mission, the young Malraux seems actually to have staged an international fraud in his own personal interest and was imprisoned by government authorities in Saigon. What we presently know of the episode is partly based on newspaper reports that have been unearthed and researched, but also remains partly colored by the account given by Clara Goldschmidt Malraux in her undoubtedly romantizized memoirs.

According to Clara, one day in the summer of 1923, her husband suggested that they travel to an area of the Siam-Cambodia border once known as "the royal way," make off with some antique Khmer statues, sell them to a rich American, and live comfortably off the proceeds for a few years. In this version, Malraux's proposal sounds as offhand and capricious as Scott Fitzgerald deciding he and Zelda take a dip in the fountain in front of the Plaza Hotel. But Malraux, however *farfelu* and unpredictable he liked to portray himself, was no mere prankster. With all the aplomb of an accomplished charlatan, he succeeded in arming himself with assorted credentials that would give their mission an "official" stamp, and on 13 October they boarded ship at Marseille for the month-long voyage to Saigon.

Accompanied by a friend, Louis Chevasson, the couple organized a sort of amateur safari and set forth on the ancient "royal way." Almost miraculously, since Malraux's archeological knowledge was that of a pure dilettante, they found the remains of the temple of Banteai-Srey, proceeded to strip and load for transport seven huge stones that portrayed in bas-relief two Indochinese dancers. As in an MGM thriller, the trio and their $100,000 booty were seized on 24 December by colonial officials—and De Gaulle's future Minister of Cultural Affairs found himself under arrest.

What had actually prompted the adventure? Malraux's amateur interests had made him aware of recent discoveries and developments in that part of the world. Having attended Parisian exhibitions of Indochinese art, and also performances of a visiting Indochinese dance troupe, Malraux had begun to evidence an authentic interest in the east. Some biographers contend that Malraux was "studying" or attending lectures at the Oriental Institute in Paris. There is also some reason to believe that he had invested, and lost, a considerable sum of money in a Mexican stock venture, and sought to make a "quick killing" on the antique market, as Clara suggests. Along with the desire for adventure, a scholarly interest, and the possibility for financial gain, Malraux seems to have conceived the Cambodian adventure in a spirit of defiance and revolt.

He knew perfectly well that such art treasures are regarded as government property, but he chose to defy the law and its underlying principles. To his way of thinking, the Banteai-Srey temple lay unrestored and in ruins; its statuary was the rightful property of anyone who chose to brave the jungle and break the law in order to discover it. Malraux's code of ethics had been molded in his reading of Nietzsche where the individual is supreme. It was a magnificent gamble, but for the moment, the gambler had lost. Initially sentenced to three years' imprisonment, he finally received in an appeal trial, a one year sentence—suspended. But what of the booty, the money, the dream? Though these were gone, Malraux had meanwhile achieved not only notoriety but an unexpected "prestige" in Parisian literary circles, and at the same time linked his immediate destiny to the east.

News of Malraux's first trial had reached Paris. It became even more newsworthy when André Breton, leader of the burgeoning surrealist movement, published an article asking French intellectuals to rally to the defense of this gifted writer whose actions he saw only as the capricious prank of an adventurous young spirit. Within a few weeks, a petition did appear in Malraux's behalf, signed by twenty-three literary figures including Breton himself, André Maurois, publisher Gaston Gallimard, and such diverse personalities as Catholic novelist François Mauriac and the future communist apologist Louis Aragon. One cannot say what effect this document may have had on the Saigon appeal court; what is more interesting is the way in which the "lost gamble" paid off for André Malraux.

The author of a single inconsequential volume and a handful of articles, he had now become a celebrity. The "pope of surrealism" had publicly acclaimed him as a talented writer. Even more surprisingly, he was awarded a contract with publisher Bernard Grasset to write three books. One of these, although not the first to be published, would be *La Voie Royale*, his fictionalized adaptation of the Cambodian adventure.

La Voie Royale is the tale of two men in the Cambodian jungle: Claude Vannec, a French archeologist in his twenties, Perken, a "graying" international adventurer of German-Danish origin whose age and first name are never made known. Claude, having already published some scholarlly articles, has concocted a scheme for pillaging the art treasures of ruined temples and selling them for profit. Perken, a long-time expatriate in the east, is casting about for money to buy machine guns. This unlikely pair seems clearly fated to meet.

Before teaming up, the two take advantage of their slow voyage on shipboard to know one another better. Claude's story is simple; there really is none yet. A fledgling "conqueror," he nurtures a fierce desire to penetrate a fallen civilization and know the personal triumph of extracting works of artistic and financial value that lie buried there. Like a boy scout on his first serious expedition, he clutches and pores over his map of the "royal way," which recent reports reveal to be a source of unexplored wonders. On meeting Perken, he is fascinated, indeed "obsessed" by this legendary personage whom many of the passengers, even the captain, have been talking about so avidly.

By way of contrast to Claude's hot young enthusiasm, his tense nervous drive, and raw energy, Perken seems the model of cool, calm self-control. This side of cynical, he is widely experienced in the ways of life, knowledgeable in the ways of the east, and generally skeptical, particularly with regard to joining a tyro in a "treasure island" adventure.

Ironically, Perken's own life emerges in the telling as a far more flamboyant adventure tale than Claude's plot for invading the jungle in search of statuary. At some point, he had succeeded in subduing a tribe of native savages, becoming their "white chief;" it is this aspect of his legend that Claude has heard vaguely murmured on shipboard. Perken had once harbored a dream of leading "his people" in combat against other tribes and/or colonial invaders. Now that dream has died, killed by the lucid recognition that modern civilization will inevitably penetrate his kingdom. A new self-defensive dream has supplanted the earlier one: with modern weapons—machine guns—Perken can perhaps arrest the encroachments of radios and railroads, the paper bureaucracy, "civilization."

As part of the deal with Claude (they are to share equally the proceeds of the booty), Perken is insistent that they continue somewhat beyond the limits of the "royal way" in search of a fellow adventurer, Grabot. An army deserter, Grabot had gone forth alone into jungle territory and, like Perken, subdued a savage tribe. His legend, however, is far more exotic than Perken's, and has come to haunt Perkens, as it will increasingly haunt Claude as well.

Defiance and will power are Grabot's essential character traits. In an act of hollow vengeance over an army doctor who had refused to admit him to the hospital, Grabot has taken his own gonorrhea discharge and blinded himself in one eye. His immediate whereabouts are unknown. Speculating on Grabot (whom he has known slightly, and apparently envied and emulated), Perken dismisses such obvious activities as trafficking in arms or gold; these are for the common adventurer. Grabot's mission is not one of self-aggrandizement alone but one of self-fulfillment, the encounter with his own destiny. To Perken, Grabot is an example of individualism and courage of a kind pushed to their outermost limits. He explains to Claude, not without admiration, Grabot's "revolver theory."

Grabot does not fear death as an abstraction; he fears the act of "being killed." Death is not only inevitable but even prematurely likely for the adventurer-conqueror who, by definition, is challenging death. It is the ultimate *humiliation* of not controlling one's destiny—meeting death at the hands of savage nature or at the hands of one's fellow man, savage or civilized—that torments Grabot. And so one bullet in his revolver always remains unfired, reserved for the dignity of suicide.

Perken's motives in seeking out Grabot are not fully clear. Does he mean to take measure of the man as a rival tribe leader, or is their encounter to be merely a verification that Grabot still exists, a key to Perken's own future? With cool lucidity, as the jungle heat bears more fiendishly down on him and Claude, Perken considers the possibilities: Grabot is either dead or alive; if alive, fully in command of his powers or—he "may have gone savage himself." This last notion intrigues the novice Claude.

Claude's apprenticeship in the business of becoming a man is a redoubtable one. As with almost all of Malraux's early heroes, it is his will to conquer that drives him on. The more deeply their caravan penetrates into jungle, the less visible the "royal way" becomes. The logic and design of Claude's map, which is all he had known of the territory, has become the brute and brutal reality of vile vegetation, insects, and vermin, "things that ooze and things that crawl." A cultivated Parisian (like Malraux himself) and a young man of heightened sensibilities (again like the young Malraux), Claude Vannec is singularly ill-equipped to cope with this world he has boldly chosen to challenge.

The pages describing this jungle treasure hunt are masterfully composed; they bathe in a bizarre poetry and exude an unwonted heroic lyricism. In this nightmarish universe, spiders, ants, termites, and worms are the ruling population. An occasional toad or lizard is half-seen darting through the underbrush. Unseen monkeys crack branches. But above all, it is an insect kingdom. Insect and vegetal. Claude reacts with equal horror and revulsion to the inanimate moss and the dank, frothy slime with which his body constantly comes into contact. Buried beneath that world, however, lie monuments of a civilization and, for Claude, the ecstasy of discovery, the reward of money, and the triumph of a personal conquest.

Progress toward that goal is predictably suspenseful. They pass dangerously close to a hostile tribe, ceremoniously burying its dead. They come upon temples with no evidence of statuary, unfinished temple structures, temples totally in ruins. Finding at last the one temple with bas-reliefs worthy of their search, they begin the battle to disengage the stones. Claude's stone-saw breaks. Later, some of their frightened native guides run off and abandon them.

Such narrative devices, now wearily, almost laughably familiar to film-goers and TV viewers, were not yet clichés half a century ago. Compressed to the form of bare plot outline, they smack unduly of melodrama. In effect, although elements of the gothic and Grand Guignol are sporadically present in Malraux's novels, his style is commendably restrained and understated. It is the moral and philosophical substance, the human import beneath the surface action, that dominates Malraux's fiction, and that is what the serious reader retains.

Claude's struggle to extricate the statuary is B movie fare. Even its most blatantly obvious meaning—man triumphs over obstacle—is little better than facile Nick Carter heroism. Within the overall context of the novel, however, it is a bold assertion of the will to power, one of the book's key themes. The moment when Claude and Perken load these precious, beautifully carved stones, testaments to the distant, almost legendary Khmer civilization, is a moment of solemn victory.

Like legendary figures themselves, doomed to yet another Herculean labor, they push on in search of Grabot. "Has he perhaps turned savage himself?" The question incessantly troubles and torments Claude. Outside Perken's calculations, however, there is a possibility unforeseen. They find Grabot in a hostile native village where the once mighty, godlike European lord is now held prisoner by Moi tribesmen. Slave rather than captive, he has been awarded as a "possession" to one of the warriors who keeps him inside a hut, bound to a treadmill, totally blind, for they have gouged out his other eye. Their attempt to interrogate him, once given the natives' reluctant consent, is futile, rewarded by only animal-like grunts. As Claude and Perken turn to leave, the dehumanized Grabot mechanically resumes his endlessly circular treadmill march.

Perken's daring ruse to "save" Grabot is, ironically, rooted in that mock-heroic courage which Grabot's present state shows to be hollow. In the most gripping moment of the episode, Perken walks directly and defiantly toward the assembled tribesmen, his bravura virtually hypnotizing them into inaction. With unswerving command, he succeeds in bargaining for Grabot's release. Jars for drinking whiskey are highly prized among the natives, and when Perken triumphantly exclaims "This man is worth a hundred jars!" Grabot's status as an object—a *thing*—is again confirmed.

To assure the success of his negotiations, Perken adds a superbly theatrical touch. Watching this legendary "white chief" fire his revolver at a dead animal skull, the natives are stunned to see blood flow there, all the more so when their own chief tastes it and declares that this is human blood. Perken later explains to Claude that he has filled an empty bullet shell with blood from his own wounded foot. Verging on the grotesquely comic, the scene is solemnized when Malraux's camera moves slowly in on the skull where Perken's blood has coagulated to form a shiny red drop glistening in the sun.

The adventure over, death begins. Having held his gaze relentlessly on the enemy, Perken failed to see the poisoned spearhead that has now infected his whole leg. Amputation is the only solution, and there is no one anywhere nearby competent to amputate. Thus, Malraux rather hastily summarizes his hitherto slow-paced narrative. The fate of their looted treasure is left in doubt, and even Claude has ceased to care much. Just as in *Lunes en papier*, where no one can remember why they have bothered to kill Death, triumph is hollow.

The French colonial government, which had heretofore regarded Grabot as a deserter, now invokes him as a martyr. They use the pretext of a white man being held captive to send troops against the natives. But Perken knows full well that this invasion means the advent of western civilization and the spread of colonialism: the end of his dream of "kingdom." The day of the solitary conqueror is over, and he himself is about to die.

The money, the machine guns, the power and the

glory, have all turned to the dust of illusion. One grim reality remains: the death Perken recklessly courted without ever believing in it except as a philosophic theorem. Claude, helplessly watching his friend in the throes of pain and fever, has bitterly acquired a profound and severe new concept of heroism, beyond the empty exploits of action. Perken's physical anguish, he begins to understand, is nonetheless a clutching testimony to life, a stoic defiance of death. For Perken, Death as an abstraction has assumed the most real of unreal forms: "There is no death . . . there's only me . . . me . . . about to die." As he watches his friend, Claude's desperately fraternal expression, a silent statement of brotherhood, is met by Perken's cadaverous eyes, which now see his companion only as a stranger, "a stranger from another world."

La Voie Royale is an imperfect book, suffering from a lack of sustained narrative perspective, tottering sometimes precariously at the brink of melodrama—just as life often does. Yet it sings of a kind of grandeur, the glorious possibilities of humankind, while capturing the dark chant of death's implacable presence. It is a tale of adventure told by a poet who happens also to be a philosopher: not just a good adventure tale but also a philosophic poem about death.

Faults and stylistic excesses are more than compensated for by the novel's artfully scaled four-part structure. The first section describes a meeting of adventurers; the last, their parting and the defeat of their dreams. Each of two center sections (Claude's search for treasure, Perken's symbolic search for Grabot) mirrors the other. One quest involves a buried civilization all but reclaimed by savage nature. The other symbolizes civilized man enslaved by the savage people he had set out to conquer.

The notion of the "white chief" is not so extravagant as it may sound to today's readers. There are numerous historical instances including a certain Mayrena whom Malraux mentions, along with Perken and Grabot, in his tale. One thinks, too, of the extraordinary young Briton T. E. Lawrence—Lawrence of Arabia—who joined the Arab freedom cause and, within the framework of World War I, led the Arab overthrow of Turkish dominion, becoming a kind of uncrowned "king." Malraux was understandably fascinated by this legendary conqueror, and even began a book about him.

The search for Grabot even more specifically recalls Joseph Conrad's *Heart of Darkness*, which, according to Clara Malraux, her husband had read only shortly before leaving for Cambodia. In both tales, an adventurer goes in search of another, not knowing what he will find. Conrad's story describes the horror of the white chief gone savage, that tantalizing prophecy with which Malraux teases his reader before turning to an outcome even more ironically tragic.

Irony, ever a favorite tool of Malraux, dominates *La Voie Royale*. Perken's situation is ironic in the extreme. He engages in the pillage of an ancient civilization in order to buy modern weapons to hold back the onslaught of modern civilization. He is passively reduced to watching helplessly as the troops of that civilization conquer and subdue "his" natives. His is the death of a godhead.

Grabot, the prototype conqueror, has been reduced from ruler to slave. He is stripped of force and reason, stripped even of that single redeeming bullet which we may symbolically interpret as the bullet Perken fires at the animal skull, thereby commemorating both Grabot's "salvation" and his own death. Grabot's invulnerability is quite percisely his unwavering belief in his own invulnerability. Another godhead gone.

Claude, the godlike prime mover of this extravagant expedition, ends as the passive witness to the death of a man he had loved and admired. All three adventurers, men of action, have been reduced to a state of immobility, a passivity as ponderously oppressive as that of the slow-moving ship against which Claude's jangling nerves had screamed out in an ironically prophetic statement in the novel's first section: "To get free of this life steeped in hopes and dreams, to get free of this damned passive boat!" Now he, too, has watched his dream disappear. But the Khmer statuary diminishes in significance: only the possibility of Claude's acquired wisdom tempers the ferocity of Malraux's ironic bite. The very title, *La Voie Royale*, with its gold and crimson glitter, is ironically emblematic of empty promise. Conquerors and cultures are destined to die.

3

Conquest and Death

In November 1924, after nearly a year of judicial problems, Malraux returned briefly to Paris, rejoining Clara. Originally indicted with her husband, she had been released, and once back in France had been instrumental in rounding up the enthusiasm of Breton and other writers to take up Malraux's legal cause. Quite by chance, she was also responsible for preparing the second stage of Malraux's experiences in Indochina. En route home, Clara had made the acquaintance of a young French lawyer, Paul Monin, who was actively engaged in the revolutionary politics of Indochina. With Monin's help, Malraux determined to return to Saigon and launch a liberal, anticolonial newspaper, again playing a dangerous game with the government.

In addition to a $600 "advance" from his publisher, Malraux received a modest sum from his generous but prudent father who warned him that "one failure is forgivable, a second is not." With these funds and a newly-directed enthusiasm, André and Clara Malraux, together with Paul Monin, founded their French-language *L'Indochine*. Malraux's wish to publish in the native language of the country, thereby reaching a wider and more receptive audience, had been flatly rejected by colonial officials. That he was permitted, as a convicted lawbreaker, to publish a left-wing newspaper at all is in itself surprising. In this venture, as in the temple theft, Malraux's spirit of revolt continued to flame; he was constantly at odds with the authorities.

Issues of *L'Indochine* (still available at the Versailles branch of the French National Library) do little credit to the writer or the man. However worthy one may deem his intentions—anti-colonialism, support of the downtrodden and the national independence movement—Malraux's editorials seem rather the sophomoric efforts of a spirited and vaguely "revolutionary" undergraduate bent on taunting the establishment. Malraux held no clearly defined political philosophy, no firm course of action; he was simply *there*, like a Socratic gadfly, as a nuisance to colonial officials. His attacks on them, often personal as well as political, and on the editors of rival newspapers, sound essentially childish and gratuitously vituperative, like those of a cranky Voltaire railing against the church.*

The Governor General soon had enough of this "radical" but sensed in him a potentially dangerous adversary. Instead of suppressing *L'Indochine* outright, he saw to its effective suppression by threatening Malraux's printer. With the help of friends and an old reconditioned printing press, André and Clara were determined to continue publishing on their own. They even journeyed to Hong Kong to obtain the needed lettering type; writing forty years later, Malraux would recall the episode with affection. Their newspaper was thus relaunched and dramatically rechristened *L'Indochine Enchaînée* (Indochina in Chains), but survived slightly less long than its predecessor.

During his two years in Indochina, Malraux not only had the opportunity to observe another civilization firsthand, he acquired a comparative east-west perspective that would profoundly modify his thinking and leave a dis-

---

* For a more sympathetic view of Malraux as a fighting liberal journalist, see *André Malraux: The Indochina Adventure* by Walter Langlois.

tinctive mark on his writings. As a fledgling editor-publisher, he came into contact with members of the Saigon intelligentsia and supporters of the Young Annam movement seeking greater freedom and autonomy for colonial Indochina.

Virtually by accident and personal caprice, he had stumbled onto history in the making. Although the revolutionary spirit in Indochina would not fully flare up for several decades (when names like Saigon and Pnom-penh would appear daily in world headlines of the 1960s), Malraux was in a strategic position to follow closely the events in Canton, where active revolution was brewing in the summer of 1925, and to use them as the backdrop for a novel.

Since the decline of the imperial dynasties that had ruled for centuries, China had fallen victim to two forces: the chaos of inner strife, with warlords in feudal fashion conquering provinces and ruling them by terror, and the exploitation of foreign nations, particularly Japan and Great Britain. Only a strong nationalist movement could succeed in bringing about some new form of unity, and this had reached its first coherent expression under Sun Yat-sen, president of the first Chinese republic. On Sun's death in 1925, the power of his Kuomintang party passed to Chiang Kai-shek who had achieved military and political prominence as head of the Whampoa Military Academy.

Unlike Sun, however, Chiang was anti-communist. But he was also a pragmatic realist, and willing to work with both the growing young Chinese communist party and the Soviet Union insofar as this would contribute to a nationalist victory over both warlords and foreign domination. The Soviet Union, although its own revolutionary communist government was only a few years old, had been opportunistically quick to seize upon the unrest in China and to convert the situation to its own design for world revolution and world marxism, Moscow-style.

Soviet "advisors" (a familiar euphemism of our

own era) were increasingly present in various capacities: training officers along with Chiang at the Whampoa Academy, indoctrinating young Chinese as revolutionary organizers, and also acting as liaison between the Kremlin and the Kuomintang. Chinese communist policy was at that time decreed by Moscow, and dictated by a young party bureaucrat named Josef Stalin. The leading Soviet emissary in China from 1923 to 1927 was Mikhail Borodine whose assignment was to reorganize the Kuomintang along Soviet lines and infiltrate the nationalist party with communist strength. In order to give his novel, *Les Conquérants*, an authentic documentary flavor, Malraux used the device of introducing actual historical figures, among them, Borodine. Along with Garine, the fictional hero of the novel, Borodine faces the practical task of agitating the already restless Chinese workers and trying to consolidate them into a viable force of activists.

The early 1920s, particularly in the southern Chinese cities of Canton and British-controlled Hong Kong, were marked by labor strikes. In a pattern familiar to political observers of the later twentieth century, such strikes invariably produced violence, leading to the death of workers who, in turn, became "martyrs." The resulting propaganda naturally served to provoke further strikes and demonstrations, enlisting more and more supporters to the revolutionary cause. Such was the seething situation in the late spring and early summer of 1925, when, on June 23, British and French troops killed more than fifty demonstrators in Canton.

Taking advantage of the situation, the revolutionary coalition succeeded in enforcing a sixteen-month boycott of Hong Kong harbor with the intention of eliminating foreign trade and asserting its combined nationalist-communist power.

Such was the immediate historical backdrop against which André Malraux set *Les Conquérants*, which centers on the European Garine, who has gone to China to work for the revolution. He is neither a mercenary in the conventional sense, though he is paid for his services, nor is he an ardently involved volunteer, selflessly throwing himself into a cause. Garine professes not to care deeply about the mission to which he is committed; he sees it rather as a necessary project for the process of self-fulfillment, a way of giving his own life meaning.

What Garine is and *why* he is there provide the focus of Malraux's pseudo-documentary study. Garine's psychology and his starkly singular concept of the meaning of life and death are ultimately more interesting than the historical events that inspired the novel, and it is clear that Malraux intended this effect on the reader. Thus, while *Les Conquérants* is a grippingly narrated slice of twentieth-century history, and also the fascinating portrait of an enigmatic man, it emerges above all as a profound and original view of man's destiny. A decade before existentialism even began to take form, Malraux had brought into question the concept of existential being.

The novel is told in the first person by a nameless, self-effacing narrator, resembling a little the narrator of Christopher Isherwood's *Berlin Stories* who calls himself "a camera." An old if not close friend of Garine, he has come to serve in the bureau of revolutionary propaganda, but his fictional function is essentially to act as author's intermediary in creating a composite view of Garine.

The style of *Les Conquérants* is consciously anti-literary. Although Malraux's later works are laced with passages of lyricism, here he favors a tough, almost telegraphic prose, and a somewhat excessive penchant for incomplete, verbless sentences. If mannered, this is at least an appropriate mannerism, for the men he was describing were violent men, acting out a violent experience, and Malraux was also seeking the crisp, detached flavor of documentary.

Les Conquérants is a short novel in three parts covering a period of six weeks during the summer of 1925. Each section is subdivided into fragmentary segments bearing designations such as "15 June," "the next morning," "5 July, 5 o'clock," "9 o'clock anchored off Hongkong," creating the effect of a diary or newspaper, and immersing the reader in a succession of rapid-fire events with the illusion of actual participation. Crisp notations—"8 August. Hong was arrested last night!"—punctuate longer descriptive and narrative passages.

The entire first section of the novel is devoted to an accumulation of data concerning Garine. The narrator is on shipboard in the Indian Ocean, en route for Canton. The wireless brings news of a general strike in Canton and an attack there by cadets of the Whampoa Military Academy under the command of Russian officers. As he stops off briefly in Saigon and Hong Kong, the narrator acquires "inside" details of the revolutionary uprising in progress; since Garine is frequently mentioned in these reports, we become increasingly acquainted with this complex, curious personage and his role. As propaganda director for the Kuomintang, assisting the Russian organizer Borodine, Garine has had great success in recruiting revolutionaries. Borodine had previously used the strict Marxist line, preaching to China's workers and peasants that they were a "great force for the new state." Counter to that abstract political metaphysic, Garine has stressed to them their importance as *individuals*, their personal human dignity. Although alien to the traditional Chinese temperament, this idea has been evoking an enthusiastic reception among the young. According to one of the narrator's informants, "The coolies are in the process of discovering that they exist, simply that they exist." Now Borodine, essentially a man of action, is occupied with converting Garine's ideological recruits into activists.

From another source, the narrator learns two more vital facts. While Borodine and Garine work well enough as a team in a common cause, there is a philosophical rift between them: Garine being more devoted to the Chinese revolution as such, Borodine owing his fidelity to Moscow. Secondly, Garine's work is taking its physical toll; suffering from a tropical ailment, he is beginning "to look like a ghost."

Back on shipboard, on the final lap of his trip, the narrator retires to his cabin and examines a confidential police docket on Garine. As he reads it through, he confirms or contradicts the facts as he knows them. Through this narrative device, like a scenario writer preparing his hero's appearance, Malraux completes this preliminary sketch of a foreign revolutionary in China.

For example, the narrator ridicules the police description of Garine as a "militant anarchist." He recalls Garine as a student in Paris, attending political meetings, but indifferent to any and all systems—including anarchy itself. A cynical youth, he derided the self-righteousness of most revolutionaries who claimed to be working for humanity. Staunchly individualist, Garine believed in a kind of Nietzschean will to power, and was greatly impressed by such heroes as Napoleon and Saint-Just, one the most ardent revolutionaries of 1789, who was spartanly "virtuous" in doctrine, yet ruthless in his ambitions. One of the most frequently quoted lines from *Les Conquérants* is Garine's bold declaration, "I want to leave a scar on the map."

Before allying himself with the uprisings in China, Garine has made various futile efforts toward self-definition. At the time of World War I, he joined the French Foreign Legion, then deserted because he seemed destined to see no battle action. Retreating to his native Switzerland, he turned to unsuccessful financial speculation. From this adventure in personal capitalism, he moved paradoxically to a flirtation with the new communism. A multilingual translator, he came into contact with international party members; with some misgiving on their part, he was admitted to occasional "cell discussions."

When the Russian revolution broke out in 1917, his colleagues left, one by one, for Moscow; Garine, still seeking action in a cause, longed to join them but possessed no authentic revolutionary credentials. Finally, a year later, he succeeded in obtaining his present post with the Kuomintang.

More than any other experience, however, Garine is haunted by the memory of his one outright encounter with the law. As a young man, he had contributed money to help pregnant girls get abortions, was arrested, and brought to trial. This confrontation with establishment ethics, so alien to his own, triggered Garine's inevitable alienation from the body social. While admitting his technical guilt, he saw the judicial process in terms of the Absurd. In his eyes, "the act of judging supposes a lack of comprehension, for if one understood, one could no longer claim to judge." Claiming total liberty as his rightful habitat, he could not even conceive of himself in prison. Yet he is emotionless when his sentence is suspended by the judge. He has written to the narrator (and here again Malraux anticipates the discourse of existentialism): "I don't find society to be bad, yet capable of being bettered; I find it to be absurd."

The action of *Les Conquérants*, although seething in an atmosphere of violence, is classically compact in the telling. Garine, having helped to effect the workers' strikes, which hold both Canton and Hong Kong paralyzed, is now pursuing a more permanent and far-reaching measure. In order to totally cripple the British Crown Colony of Hong Kong, a decree has been issued that no ship docking there will henceforth be permitted into the Chinese port of Shanghai. Virtually obsessed by the idea of halting all foreign trade, and by the feeling of power this excites in him, Garine finds himself frustrated. Not by the "enemy" British, whose strategy is at least predictable, but by the ever-voluble factionalism among his revolutionary allies.

The nationalist Kuomintang is divided not only into radical and conservative wings, it is infiltrated by communists who await Moscow's decisions before acting, and so the decree decision is delayed day after day. Malraux is clearly saying, as he will again and again, that the Soviet bureaucracy acts only in self-interest with callous disregard for world revolution. Garine is a solitary figure struggling against two empires: the British and the Russian.

His decree is further threatened by the unofficial party of Tcheng-Dai, a national hero who champions nonviolent resistance so that his conscience forbids cooperation with the Kuomintang. Without his support as well as Russia's, Garine—like Hong Kong on strike—remains paralyzed. At the opposite pole of Tcheng-Dai's pacifism, Garine is also faced with terrorists, who, though working ostensibly with the Kuomintang, will not submit to discipline and go about Canton murdering whom they choose as they choose. Surrounded by inaction and anarchy, Garine doggedly attempts to pursue his course.

This conflict of goals, policies and personalities within the tension of revolution gives Malraux the opportunity to investigate a variety of human temperaments. Like Dostoyevsky in his novel of revolution, *The Possessed*, Malraux is less concerned with plot than in contrasting a gallery of portraits: the radically divergent psychologies that drive men, even potential enemies, to band together—if only for a brief historical moment—in a fragile common cause.

Although the historical figure Borodine appears only in two short scenes, his imposing presence is felt throughout. He is seen as a man of action, but not as a free agent like his opposite number Garine. Borodine personifies the crisp, unflinching bureaucrat of the Internationale, concerned with the mechanics and the efficient administration of the revolution. "Too human" is his stock pejorative phrase for those who show feeling or emotion. Faced with intellectual abstractions, Borodine reacts like an American business tycoon: "The Revolution means meeting a payroll." In Garine's view, Borodine wants to "mass-produce revolutionaries just as Ford produces cars on the assembly line."

One of Garine's lieutenants, like his chief Borodine, is also a Russian. But Nicolaeff is an "adventurer" in the cheapest sense of the word. His portrait suggests the now familiar degenerate opportunist (Nazi, communist, or other) who will work for the side that pays. Nicolaeff, with the title of police commissioner, is a fat pig of a brute who exudes obscenity in his very being as well as in his morality. He has made his way across continents and revolutions as a spy, informer, double agent, and sometime salesman of dirty postcards. Like Garine, he enjoys power, but in an almost physical, rather than metaphysical way. In charge of an interrogation, safely surrounded by guards with drawn pistols, he takes a sadistic pleasure in contemplating the mounting fear and cowardice of the victims brought before him.

One of the most sympathetic among these "conquerors" is Klein, a German with the body of a boxer and a cultivated intellect. Even when totally drunk, he discourses with great lucidity on the theses indigenous to Malraux's world: justice, integrity, murder, liberty, suicide. Somewhere in his past there is the legendary glory of his having assassinated a Russian noble.

Not all the key figures in *Les Conquérants* are foreign adventurers, however. As the novel gains momentum, despite the intense focus on Garine's personal drama, two Chinese come increasingly to the fore: the terrorist Hong and the "saintly" pacifist, Tcheng-Dai. Generally believed to have been modeled on a young Indochinese Malraux had known during his publishing days, Hong is a compelling character whose single-minded nihilism is at once his strength and his weakness.

Born and raised in total poverty (a Cantonese poverty of the early twentieth century that few Americans can even imagine), he has been exposed to western revolutionary literature before knowing anything about his oriental heritage. Indeed, all he has known about his own civilization is oppressive hunger and degradation. Alternately educated by Jesuists and anarchists, he has learned to read French and English but not Chinese ideographs. He is the torn product of two cultures and two societies, and it is little wonder that he cannot live with himself except by striking angrily outside himself, by killing. He has become so steeped in hatred of the bourgeoisie that anything even smacking of order is anathema to him. Ironically, the opposing enthusiasms instilled in him have only turned him into a brute. A fine young sensibility has been molded into a Frankenstein monster.

Having been imbued with the Christian notion, alien to the Oriental mentality, of the importance of one's individual self, Hong has dedicated his life to the destruction of others: "Your own life. Not to lose it. That's all." Under Garine's guidance and surveillance, Hong briefly seemed capable of channeling his hate into positive concerted action, but the damage had already been done. Hong repeatedly expresses his malevolent disdain of those who "want to set things right." He does not want things set right; he wants a universal chaos in which each man takes his own vengeance and destroys. Society, any state of social organization, is "so much crap" to Hong, and so nihilism, in its most desperate form, that of terrorism, becomes his sole domain.

Although Garine can understand Hong's mentality and tries to temper his anarchistic bent, he has little use for the venerated Tcheng-Dai, a self-appointed successor to Sun Yat-sen. In general outline, the fictional Tcheng-Dai resembles the historical Mahatma Gandhi, whose program of passive resistance was instrumental in attaining India's independence from Great Britain. Garine not only opposes Tcheng-Dai politically, he imputes the Chinese leader's motives; he sees him as something of a fraud, studiously creating a legend around his person. Tcheng-Dai seeks to incarnate the "soul" of the Chinese people, and is so devoted to "justice" as an abstraction that he has come to prefer the *ideal* of his cause to its actual realization. He has, in short, the makings of a martyr. When Garine exclaims "Dear God! Deliver us from saints!" one recalls Bernard Shaw's demonstration in *Saint Joan* that saints can indeed be troublesome.

By pitting the anarchist Hong against the pacifist Tcheng-Dai at a moment of revolutionary crisis, Malraux creates an intellectual situation more tensely dramatic than the scenes of street fighting, political rallies, torture, and murder, which almost fade into the background. Tcheng-Dai demands an end to terrorism. Hong bitterly loathes "do-gooders" like Tcheng. He would wipe out, almost single-handedly, all those who preach charity. Garine's genuine affection for this desperate boy is overridden, however, by cynical pragmatism. He counts on Hong to murder Tcheng-Dai, thereby eliminating one key problem. In any case, he would rather have Hong working with him than against him.

When word comes of Tcheng-Dai's death, the propagandist in Garine moves into swift action. He learns that Tcheng's followers are papering the streets with posters of his "suicide." Whether it *was* murder or suicide is beside the revolutionary point; it is a question of which side gets the martyr! With cool dispatch, Garine orders posters blaming the British for Tcheng-Dai's death and inciting the people to revenge. As a crowning ironic and hypocritical touch to the scheme, Garine delivers an eloquent oration at Tcheng-Dai's funeral.

A bloody chain of events has been unleashed, however. Hong must be found and brought to task. This done, Hong's terrorists capture Klein and several of Garine's men, torture and kill them. Borodine, in turn, has Hong executed. Yet Garine—perhaps "too human"—is not guiltless, for he has, in effect, been gambling with other men's lives.

Garine's own death now seems imminent. Having expended all his energy in "becoming himself," he has become a walking cadaver; his physical forces spent, the fierce fire of his will all but burned out, he succumbs to the tropical disease that has plagued him. The final pages of *Les Conquérants* take on the solitary grandeur of tragedy: "There is nothing quite so simple as a man about to die."

One of the novel's singular achievements is the way in which Malraux wins our sympathy for this cynical, arrogant, essentially self-serving "conqueror." Garine assumes that he is right, and that right makes might. Smugly godlike, he requires that his will be done. Yet, in a final conversation with the narrator, the communist Nicolaeff sees Garine as just another cog in the machine, easily replaced. To him, as a soldier of the new society, this supremely individualistic adventurer is one of the last of a dying breed.

As Garine packs up to leave China, he tries to convince himself that his condition is not fatal. He keeps repeating that he will soon come back to "finish up." The reader is aware that it is Garine who is "finished." And Garine, like Perken in *La Voie Royale*, cannot help but be aware of this himself. Although *Les Conquérants* was published first, it is almost certain that Malraux had begun writing *La Voie Royale* earlier. The eruption of significant developments in Canton in 1925 may have prompted him to drop the jungle tale and take advantage of a timely event by writing a fictionalized documentary of the Chinese revolution.

Comparing Garine and Perken as conqueror types, it is obvious that Perken is a more primitive and "purer" version, a thoroughgoing egotist. Both men want to "leave a scar on the map"—to do something that will give shape and meaning to their lives and insure perhaps a small measure of immortality. Both men defy not only the existing order but any form of authority. Pointing to a colony of termites, swarming endlessly about their mounds, Perken remarks that they are destined and bound to their tiny universe: "I refuse to be bound." Garine, although working with communists, rejects marxism and its doctrinaire authority, but has at least chosen to discover his own destiny within the framework of a movement involving his fellow man.

In some ways, *La Voie Royale* and *Les Conquérants* seem one and the same book. They share, to a remarkable degree, the same underpinnings of thematic structure. This implies no dearth of creative imagination, but strongly indicates the nature of Malraux's obsessions during the Indochina period and immediately thereafter. Both novels open on shipboard, with a younger, inexperienced man about to join a seasoned adventurer in a mission of conquest. The principals in each instance have turned their backs on traditional European patterns of civilization. Their journey completed, mission accomplished with apparent success, the chief protagonist is ironically doomed to death. The final scenes are virtually identical, conveying a profound, unspoken sense of man's fraternity.

The "voyager" clearly suggests Malraux himself, moving from west to east in search of self-realization and a reappraisal of cultural and philosophical values. In his later novels, both the master-disciple relationship and the theme of universal brotherhood will continue to reappear, assuming vaster dimensions. Malraux now leaves behind the adventurer-conqueror—though not without reluctance and nostaligia—to explore destiny's new man. And man's new destiny. He will abandon the gaudy crimson and gold of conquest to portray the shadowy prison of man's fate and the pale distant light of man's hope.

4

Candy and Cyanide

When *Les Conquérants* was published in 1928, critics generally praised the novel for its stark power and boldly original interrogation of man's destiny. Some admired its effective "reporting," although we now know that Malraux had not actually witnessed the events of which he wrote, and that *Les Conquérants* is an example of history transformed through creative invention and philosophical insight. Ironically, the novel lost out on one of the foremost French literary prizes because the judges did not completely regard it as a "work of the imagination."

Les Conquérants was nonetheless a critical and commercial success. Few young writers have been so honored; a forum of illustrious critics and intellectuals devoted one of their meetings to a discussion of Garine as a problematical new breed of hero. At a later date, the novel again created a stir when Leon Trotsky wrote an article praising its merits, but with the reserve that the author and his hero both needed "a good dose of marxism." Which was precisely the medicine that Malraux refused to swallow. But it was no small honor to be involved in controversy with one of the leaders of the Russian revolution!

Trotsky commended Malraux for his authentic sensitivity to the revolutionary cause, but chastened the book's "excesses of individualism," without understanding that Malraux himself was putting the "conqueror" mentality on trial. With considerable perception into Malraux's psyche, Trotsky detected a certain "Machiavellianism" in a writer who could let himself be fascinated by such pseudo-revolutionaries as Garine. Trotsky was also among those who fell into the trap of regarding *Les Conquérants* as a chronicle of revolution rather than a novel. In his reply, Malraux denied that the book was a "fictionalized chronicle," insisting that his primary intention was to bring into perspective and to focus on "la condition humaine"—the fundamental metaphysical state of humankind, man's mortal fate and destiny.

On his return from Indochina early in 1926, Malraux had been worn and haggard from his experience there; he worked only intermittently as a free-lance editor. Now, with his career assured, André and Clara Malraux took to frequent travel. In the summer of 1928, they "discovered" Persia, and were captivated by its civilization and art. Four years in a row they would return there, along with other far-flung trips to Russia, India, the United States, and China. Aside from his very brief visit to Hong Kong in search of type for his newspaper, Malraux did not see China until 1929. While he was writing *Les Conquérants*, however, China once more became the scene of a dramatic chain of events which would provide Malraux with material for the novel that is generally regarded as his finest: *La Condition humaine*, again centering on the communist-nationalist struggle.

The Chinese communist party, numbering only about one hundred in 1922, had grown massively by 1926 into a vital force including 30,000 members, supported by innumerable non-member sympathizers. While intellectuals formed the backbone of the party, every effort was made to enlist the enthusiasm and the services of workers and peasants, as in *Les Conquérants*. Young Chinese in great numbers went off to Moscow for study in Marxist doctrine and training in the tactics of world revolution. A sizable community of Chinese and Indochinese revolutionaries was also to be found in Paris; among them, Chou En-lai, who would later become premier under Mao Tse-tung.

In March 1927, the communists and Chiang Kai-shek's Kuomintang continued to form an "uneasy alliance," with the common goal of seizing power by destroying the existing regime, but each side was also bent on destroying the other. There was a struggle within the struggle, and this was the dramatic setting for *La Condition humaine*. In April, Chiang made his move. Sensing his military and political strength at their peak, he staged a swift and bloody coup in Shanghai, arresting and murdering countless communists, and effectively repressing the party's accumulated power. Ex-banker Chiang would henceforth rule as dictator.

Depending on one's politics, this maneuver may be seen as a necessary repression, aimed at checking Soviet expansionism, or as a betrayal of the Chinese revolution, which Trotsky would call "the strangled revolution." Malraux's sympathies at the time were clearly with the revolutionaries whose aspirations had been thwarted. Twenty years later, in 1947, when Chiang was ousted by Mao's communist troops, Malraux commented with greater detachment: "The events of which I wrote then have ultimately come to pass."

In *La Condition humaine*, Malraux uses the same stylistic and structural technique that had proved so successful and so well suited to his intentions in *Les Conquérants*. He takes a brief crucial moment in history and, mixing fact with fiction, creates a tale charged with action and violence that is also a metaphysical discourse on man: the meaning of his life and the meaning of his death.

We find here again the journalistic "dateline" technique; chapter headings like "22 March/11 a.m." not only lend a documentary flavor, they create for the reader the urgency of time—time rapidly passing, time running out. As in *Les Conquérants*, Malraux tells his story and formulates his philosophical reflections by tracing the rise and fall of a handful of characters engaged in revolutionary activity. It is a gallery of portraits: men banded together in a common cause, but from different backgrounds, of different temperaments, and whose idealism is their undoing. They are caught up in a human drama that far transcends its immediate historical backdrop.

The opening situation of *La Condition humaine* also recalls that of *Les Conquérants*. As Chiang's Kuomintang forces move towards military victory, their communist "allies" in Shanghai have been ordered to stage a workers' strike and insurrection that will cripple the city. Kyo Gisors, half French and half Japanese, has been named to lead the insurrection, and it is he who may be considered the novel's chief protagonist, although he is less vividly dramatized than several of the other leading characters. The fact of Kyo's mixed parentage defines him as an "outcast," yet there is nothing of the romantic hero about him. Nor does he resemble the cold, self-centered and opportunistic heroes of Malraux's first two novels. Kyo burns with a steady flame, consumed with dedication to that simplest of "causes:" his fellow man.

By way of contrast, Tchen, a pure Chinese, is a young man on fire who chooses terrorism as his weapon against destiny, thereby creating chaos in the heart of an organized resistance and ultimately destroying himself. He is the counterpart to Hong in *Les Conquérants*, a richer, more subtly drawn portrait of the anarchist psychology that is one of Malraux's obsessions. One of the most celebrated pages of twentieth-century fiction is the opening scene of *La Condition humaine*, where Tchen kills a sleeping man. In the Shanghai night, horns honk and a pale patch of light from the street illuminates Tchen as he stands over a sleeping body from which he is separated by a mosquito net. His sole reality is the cold metal of his knife and the flesh of his victim; by some geometry of the will, he must establish the necessary contact between his knife and that flesh. To test the resistance of human flesh, Tchen first plunges the knife into his own arm. His sense of life at that moment is ironically reduced to the terrible awareness of his own mortality.

The passage is memorable not only for its dramatic tension but because it blends so remarkably two opposing modes: the metaphysical and the melodramatic. It is only after empathizing with Tchen's anguish that we learn the purpose of his act. The murdered man was in possession of a bill of sale that will enable the Shanghai insurgents to acquire an arms shipment that is waiting in the harbor. Malraux, a master of ironic juxtaposition, has almost imperceptibly shifted our perspective from a speculation on death into the "B" movie world of false passports, spies and counter-spies, machine guns in the streets.

Throughout Malraux's work, irony rules relentlessly. The bill of sale that Tchen delivers to Kyo is marked "payable on delivery," and the revolutionaries are without funds. The episode that follows once again skillfully weaves two opposites: melodrama and farce. Kyo's scheme is to board the ship under pretense of purchasing the weapons and then to overtake the crew. To establish negotiations with the captain, he enlists the services of Baron de Clappique, an international ne'er-do-well who knows everyone in Shanghai and everything that happens there. Clappique is perhaps Malraux's most formidable creation, so fascinating that more than once he threatens to dominate the novel. He is a clown of Shakespearian proportions, a schemer who is at once canny and clumsy, skilled in chicanery and wholly undependable. Malraux's absurdist view of life is such that the revolution finds itself for the moment at the mercy and the whim of an irresponsible eccentric. For Clappique is what the French call a *mythomane*, one so obsessed with lies and exaggeration that he substitutes myth for reality and can no longer distinguish between them. No matter how he is dressed, Malraux tells us, the Baron always seems to be "in disguise."

Kyo finds the Baron at the Black Cat Café, jazz playing in the background, spinning fabulous yarns before an audience of two prostitutes, ordering champagne for them and a "ver-r-r-r-y" dry martini for himself. ". . . . the great misfortune, my dear girl," we hear the Baron say, "is that there's no spirit of fantasy left in life." This is the man on whom the insurrection and countless men's lives depend. Later, Clappique again plays a life-and-death role in this revolution which is of no personal concern to him and in which he has become involved only to help Kyo. The arms shipment has been secured, and the insurrection has proved effective. Tension mounts as Chiang's forces move towards Shanghai. The communist revolutionary faction and their Moscow mentors begin to fear Chiang's victory will bring about their repression. Having "used" them, he will turn against them. As an indication of this imminent treachery, the Baron learns from a police spy that both he and Kyo are to be arrested for their part in the arms theft, and he hastens to inform Kyo. Kyo asks for details concerning himself and the fate of the insurrectionists, and they agree to meet at midnight, again at the Black Cat.

As the hour approaches, Clappique stops off at a gambling house. In the smoke-filled room, now winning, now losing, he becomes caught up in the whirl of the roulette wheel, overcome by a dizzy fatal power that leaves him alternately feeling god-like and helpless. The relentless spinning of the wheel, the back-and-forth cadence of red and black, even and odd, reduce him to a state of immobility, outside time. Intermittently conscious of his rendez-vous with Kyo, he is nonetheless incapable of freeing himself from the fascinating, futile contest with chance that is renewed each time he wagers. By 1 a.m., he has gambled away almost all his money—and also Kyo's life.

Malraux's design here is a familiar one: the individual versus the collective, the juxtaposition of the egocentric temperament and the communal temperament. A collective action, particularly revolution, calls for unity and solidarity; as one character in *La Condition humaine* bluntly states: "If everybody goes their own way, we're screwed." The individual, at least momentarily, must surrender his own individuality. Garine was incapable of this, and while the Baron is a far cry from Garine, his is the portrait of individualism, eccentricity, and self-expression carried to their tragi-comic extreme. Such characteristics can only be a menace to all that Kyo represents, a brotherhood of self-sacrifice. The Baron, always "on stage" and playing the clown, likes to tease by saying "The Baron de Clappique does not exist!" In so doing, he unerringly identifies his existential state of self-annihilation.

Without meaning to be, Tchen is also an enemy of Kyo's and an enemy of the revolution in the sense that he goes his own way. Like Hong in *Les Conquérants*, he refuses to subscribe to any code but his own. Tchen's story, which takes up a considerable portion of *La Condition humaine*, is a study in anarchy. Having proved himself capable of killing, and with no regrets, Tchen nonetheless feels the anguish of solitude, a terrible alienation from the world of men. His comrades are too busy plotting to understand his feelings, and so he turns to Kyo Gisors's father whom he regards as his own spiritual father.

The scene bears a striking resemblance to that of a repentant sinner's confession to a priest, except that Tchen is unrepentant, and what he is "confessing" is not his crime but the inner agony from which he cannot free himself. In a sense, old Gisors is the right man for him to talk to, yet they are too temperamentally apart for the true understanding Tchen seeks. Gisors is a philosopher, a theoretician of political revolt; his radical views and certain articles he has published have cost him his professorship at the university, and this is his paper badge of courage. Tchen is a practicing terrorist. Gisors, a native European, has lived long in the east, embracing oriental ways. A mandarin-like intellectual, and also a smoker of opium, he embodies a kind of *stasis*, removed from the world of violence that Tchen has adopted. Despite Gisors's intuitive grasp of the young man's plight, the two remain worlds apart, Gisors having retreated into a circle of meditation and opium while Tchen hurls himself further into a world of violence that will end in self-destruction. With typically Malrucian irony, it was Gisors who was initially responsible for inspiring Tchen's interest in revolution.

Tchen's first murder was an act of duty; he was simply carrying out orders. When he hears that Chiang Kai-shek will almost surely turn on the communists and thwart the revolution, Tchen decides to take matters into his own hands, assuming the personal mission of murdering Chiang. With the defiant pride of the terrorist, Tchen is bent on creating his own solitary myth and martyrdom. Stationing himself in a shop on the street where Chiang's car is to pass, he waits impatiently, clutching a hidden bomb while fingering objets d'art and perfunctorily asking prices of the shopkeeper. It is a scene of nerve-wracking suspense that takes an ironic turn when the shopkeeper suspects that Tchen has stolen something and creates a disturbance that keeps him from hurling his bomb.

Later that night, he tries again, and this time succeeds in throwing his bomb against a car, ironically never knowing that it was the wrong car. For Tchen immediately kills himself by firing a bullet into his mouth before he can be captured. Tchen, who believes in terrorism as a form of total self-realization, dies a "heroic" suicide, in vain. In different ways, and in varying degrees, Gisors, the Baron, and Tchen exemplify aspects of non-conformist individualism that is not only counterproductive but virtually counterrevolutionary.

Malraux, having devoted a great many pages to these three powerful characterizations, now returns to Kyo Gisors who, up to this point, has been somewhat overshadowed and known to the reader chiefly through his relationships with others. One of those is his blonde, German-born wife May who is a physician. Theirs is a "modern" marriage, rooted in love but with such a respect for mutual independence that May, one afternoon, exercises her liberty by sleeping with a fellow doctor, not out of genuine desire but simply because he seemed to want her. May's frank, unemotional confession brings Kyo, jealous in spite of himself and disdaining his very jealousy, to speculate on the limits of human liberty, and the essential solitude of being human.

Kyo is more a man of action than his father, but more reflective in his actions than the terrorist Tchen. He is *of* this world in a vivid and tangible way, just as the Baron de Clappique and old Gisors are not. Our most frequent visualization of Kyo is that of a shadowy figure, in sweater and sneakers, moving quietly through the night. There is about him a silent restlessness, coupled with a resolute calm—a will to be "at peace with the night." In a scene often analyzed by critics, Kyo hears his own voice played back on a phonograph record and fails to recognize that voice; he is destined to be a stranger to himself. But Kyo takes the step Garine could not take; his commitment to his fellow man and to the revolutionary cause is not merely a means to self-realization but an end unto itself.

Only in the final pages of *La Condition humaine*, when he is captured by the police, beaten in the street, and thrown into prison, does Kyo play out the central role that he seemed destined to fulfill from the start. One of his fellow prisoners is a madman who keeps crying out, and is being brutalized by the guards. When Kyo asks mercy for the man, he himself is whipped for intervening. Another prisoner tells him: "I'd rather get fed in jail than starve out there free." Kyo's—and Malraux's—disdain for such men is tacitly implicit. The tense dialogue at Kyo's interrogation underscores the point:

> "You want to live?"
> "It all depends how."
> "People die different ways too."
> "But they don't have any choice in that."

With this idea of "choosing" one's life and one's destiny, it is apparent that Malraux, more than a dozen years before the wave of existentialist literature swept over the post-war world, was already formulating a credo wherein man is the sum of his acts and that we do indeed choose the acts that constitute our lives—or else, like the Baron de Clappique, cease to exist. In this powerful prison scene, there is also evidence that despite Kyo's statement, we may also choose our death.

"Death is a state of passivity, but suicide is an act." So run Kyo's thoughts as the prospect of torture, degradation, and death at the hands of others grows increasingly real. Finding the capsule of cyanide which he, like certain of his comrades, always kept with him, Kyo bites firmly down on the poison, as though he were barking out an order to his men. Tchen's more flamboyant suicide had neither the redemptive lucidity nor the deep-rooted humanity that marks Kyo's. Kyo not only affirms his dignity as an individual, he is passionately aware of the hundreds of revolutionary prisoners facing execution and the spirit of brotherhood surrounding him: "He would die among those with whom he could have wanted to live; he would die, like each of those men lying there, having given a meaning to his life. . . . It is easy to die if you don't have to die alone." At Kyo's side is his friend and fellow revolutionary, a Russian named Katow. Moved by Kyo's gesture, Katow makes an even grander gesture—that of self-sacrifice. He gives away his cyanide to two of his comrades in order to spare them the prolonged agony of torture and degradation in death that almost certainly lie in store.

Malraux was not particularly given to using "symbols," yet at the beginning of *La Condition humaine*, and again at the end of the novel, he introduces *candy* in a subtle way that seems somehow symbolic. After Tchen, in the opening scene, has killed his man, he rejoins Kyo, Katow and the others, feeling a sense of maturity and manhood. However, when he sees Katow with a bag of candy, he is consumed with childish gluttony, rather like a kid or a puppy asking for their "reward." In the final chapter, a group of French businessmen and government officials are gathered to discuss the downfall of Chinese communism and the triumph of Chiang Kai-shek's conservative bourgeois regime. Smugly content, they sit chewing caramels. Meanwhile, Tchen, Kyo, and Katow, Malraux's revolutionary "conquering heroes," have all met death as their reward. Katow's candy has turned to cyanide.

What unites Malraux's first three novels into a kind of triptych, if not trilogy, is their common view of man's destiny. And it is a tragic view, perhaps not in the strict Aristotelian sense, but in a starkly twentieth-century perspective. As in his first published tale, *Lunes en papier*, Malraux consistently depicted an absurd and godless universe with no absolute values and in which man, alone, faces the adversary death. Perken and Garine, seeking to give meaning to their lives by pursuing adventure, meet death essentially unfulfilled. Kyo and Katow represent a totally different kind of "conqueror." Although their political mission has failed, they have contributed to the aspirations of their fellow men and in a transcendant sense "conquered" death, cognizant of their own human worth and their faith in human brotherhood. The idea of "fraternity" that was suggested in *La Voie royale* and *Les Conquérants* is deeply inscribed in the pages of *La Condition humaine.*

The title of Malraux's novel derives from the seventeenth-century *Pensées* (Reflections) of Blaise Pascal. In Pascal's dark metaphor, the "human condition" is likened to the fate of prisoners who each day see one of their number murdered before their very eyes. Like Malraux's revolutionaries, they are inescapably bound to an ever-present consciousness of their own mortality. Redemption for Pascal lay in the grace of Christ and our embrace of Him. For Malraux, there is only Man.

5

Ave atque Vale

La Condition humaine first appeared serially in successive issues (January-June, 1933) of the *Nouvelle Revue Française*, the prestigious literary magazine published by Gaston Gallimard, and then in book form in Gallimard's NRF editions. A great popular and critical success, soon translated into more than a dozen languages, *La Condition humaine* won the highest national honor available to a French novelist, the Prix Goncourt.

Malraux, at 32, could now legitimately enjoy the success and fame he had less scrupulously sought a decade earlier in the jungles of Cambodia. Clara had given birth to a daughter named Florence (in commemoration perhaps of their pre-nuptial "honeymoon" in Italy), and the couple had settled into an apartment in the St. Germain des Près quarter of Paris, close by the NRF offices where Malraux also worked as an editor. The European intellectual of the early 1930s, however, could scarcely content himself with books and art when the world was about to explode. Italian fascism grew increasingly menacing as dictator Benito Mussolini proclaimed the dawn of a new Roman Empire. In March, 1933, the Berlin Reichstag ceded full power to Adolph Hitler, and Germany became a one-party state under Nazism. A massive imperialistic machine was being forged, with world conquest as its goal. Since the Soviet Union's monolithic communist party was also bent on world domination, a mighty confrontation was inevitable.

Restless by nature, and sensitive to the impending holocaust, André Malraux undertook three journeys during 1934: two of them reflecting his profound awareness of international crisis, the other seeming rather a throwback to his adolescent urge for personal adventure and "conquest." In January, with fellow NRF writer André Gide, Malraux travelled to Berlin in hopes of an audience with Hitler. Their purpose was to petition for the release from prison of a leading communist named Dimitrov. According to Malraux, they were received by Hitler's propaganda minister Goebbels who accused them of not understanding "German justice." Yet a month later, Dimitrov was freed from prison, and both Gide and Malraux continued to participate in rallies in behalf of Dimitrov's German comrade Ernst Thaelmann.

During the summer of 1934, Malraux journeyed to Moscow to participate in an international writers' conference. His companion on that trip was Paris-based Soviet journalist Ilya Ehrenburg who had written a favorable critique of *La Condition humaine*, yet reproached Malraux, as Trotsky previously had, for not grasping the true nature of social revolution. This appears to have been the official communist party attitude towards Malraux, and so he was courted by Soviet dignitaries as a spiritual ally, accorded prestige and privilege, yet held in suspicion for his outspoken views on individual liberty and, in particular, the freedom of the artist. While in Russia, he met Maxim Gorki, the aging author of *Dead Souls* and *The Lower Depths*, and was photographed with Boris Pasternak, later to achieve controversial fame through his novel, *Dr. Zhivago*. Malraux was also flattered to find several eminent filmmakers, including the illustrious Sergei Eisenstein, interested in doing a cinematic version of *La Condition humaine*, but nothing ever came of these projects.

There can be no question that André Malraux, an

ambitious young man with a taste for personal glory, greatly relished his new role as self-appointed emissary to foreign capitals in behalf of "causes." Here were vengeance and reward for the ignominy he had suffered at the hands of the official French court in Pnom-Penh. Both as crusader and writer, he had earned his credentials as a world figure of certain stature. What then was Malraux's motivation in undertaking—between the Berlin and Moscow trips—a flight over Southern Arabia in search of the "lost kingdom" of Sheba?

On 22 February, in a plane about as sturdy as Lindbergh's, Malraux set forth, with a pilot and a mechanic, for Cairo and then for Djibouti, the capital of French Somaliland which conjures memories of the legendary Arthur Rimbaud who abandoned poetry at seventeen to become an African adventurer. Wearing Arab costume (which in turn suggests T. E. Lawrence, the legendary Lawrence of Arabia), the three men succeeded in circling and photographing a topography that Malraux did not hesitate to identify as the "lost kingdom." After a sojourn in Ethiopia, soon to be invaded by Italian forces, Malraux landed back in Paris on 23 March and suffered the slight of being identified as "a passenger" by one newspaper which gave the names of his unknown fellow crew members. Ample personal publicity was provided, however, by the newspaper *l'Intransigeant* which had apparently helped subsidize the enterprise and carried a series of front page articles written by Malraux. It seems there remained in him still a taste for daredevil adventure and publicity that had not yet been satisfied by his literary reputation alone. Thirty years later, writing what he would call his "anti-memoirs," Malraux devoted a dozen dramatic pages to the Sheba flight, summing it up by saying: "Such legendary lands attract the *farfelus*," using the same curious epithet he had adopted in *Lunes en papier* to suggest crazy adventure and death-defying conquest.

Out of the disparate elements of those three 1934

journeys grew Malraux's fourth novel, *Le Temps du mépris.* Berlin and Moscow provided the basic scenario, which deals with a communist held political prisoner by the Nazis, while the "*farfelu*" Sheba adventure, in which Malraux learned first hand the intoxicating and dangerous experience of flight, generated a memorable passage where Kassner, the hero of *Le Temps du mépris*, is flown to freedom aboard a small aircraft.

In *Le Temps du mépris*, Malraux attempted a simplicity of narrative form that he had theretofore largely resisted. *Les Conquérants* and *La Condition humaine* are full-scale works of fiction, charged if not over-charged with action, and teeming with a variety of complex characters. *La Voie Royale* starts as Claude's story, becomes Perken's, yet the reader is somehow also haunted by Grabot, a character we scarcely see at all. *Le Temps du mépris*, on the contrary, maintains a sharp steady focus on one man, Kassner, whose imprisonment and deliverance from prison in about a week's time provide the sole matter of Malraux's tale. Less than a hundred pages in length, highly concentrated in time and tone, *Le Temps du mépris* is more novella than novel, though it is generally counted as one of Malraux's six "novels."

In a brief introduction, Malraux invites the reader to accept this work in terms of traditional tragedy, with two protagonists at the fore: "the hero and his concept of life." He clearly intends Kassner to be allegorical man, devoid of those individualistic traits and personal conflicts that infuse the modern novel with psychological complexity. True to his intent, Malraux has created a simple tale that partakes both of stark, brutal realism and the wondrous unreality of legend. Following the model of antique tragedy, he even provides a twentieth century *deus ex machina*: the plane that escorts his hero from prison to freedom.

Kassner is, in some ways, the recognizable progeny of Malraux's previous heroes in that he is fighting for a cause. But unlike the "conquerors," his individualism has been absorbed into the collectivity of communism and given a direction. Unlike Kyo, he is destined to triumph over prison and death; defying destiny, he becomes a true conqueror. Kassner's background is a familiar one, again reflecting elements of Malraux's life and legend, or at least the heroic mold in which he liked to cast himself.

Though German-born, Kassner has spent much of his life abroad. He has fought in World War I and in the Russian revolution; he has been trained in Moscow and spent time in the Orient. Although he appears to play some part in the clandestine communist propaganda service, his chief role, back in Germany, is that of organizing workers, and in particular, workers' strikes. Like Garine then, his primary function is to create *paralysis*, and Kassner's story is made to hinge on the dramatic opposition of two "arrests:" the anti-Nazi work stoppage he is attempting to effect and his actual capture by storm troopers which leads to the immobility of imprisonment and almost certain death.

Le Temps du mépris also plays, within its modest framework, on the theme of *identity*. If the Nazis can positively identify their prisoner as Kassner, one of the leading German communists, they can proceed to liquidate him. Kassner, however, no longer resembles the photograph they have. As his captors study the photo, Kassner in turn studies them and notes that this is the first time he has ever encountered his own "legend" on the face of the enemy. While the Nazi officers pursue the task of identification, Kassner, in the isolation of his cell, must come to grips with the basic moral problem of self-identity. Will he have the strength to endure, even in the face of torture, and resist that confession which would in turn jeopardize his comrades' lives? This triggers, at yet another level, the question of human identity that is Malraux's key theme here: the role of individual consciousness within the framework of collective action. The question had been implicit in Malraux's writing from the start. His answer, to be demonstrated as Kassner's adventure unfolds, is set forth aphoristically in the preface to *Le Temps du mépris*: "the individual stands in opposition to collective man, but is enriched by that collectivity. The nature of his opposition is less significant than the way in which he is enriched."

Kassner, an eminently social animal, is reduced to three forms of contact with the world outside his own person: the intrusion of his captors into his cell, the awareness of other prisoners in other cells, and the "presence" of prisoners past who have left inscriptions on the walls. Malraux fully exploits each potential. What Kassner dreads most is torture, the systematically calculated breakdown of one's humanity. He attempts to close his ears against the cries that come from nearby cells. Four storm troopers enter his own cell, and while two others stand watch, gratuitously beat and kick him into an unconscious state. Compared to torture, this bullying attack is almost "laughable."

From time to time, and in varying degrees, Kassner musters an iota of hope from the notion of comradeship. This takes on two forms. The graffiti on the walls of his cell bear witness to the long line of defiant prisoners who have preceded him. One reads: "Before the month is out, I'll kill Federwisch." Kassner cannot but wonder which of the two—captor or prisoner—actually survived. Of more immediate encouragement is the incessant tapping he hears on his wall, coming from the cell adjacent. He surmises a message is being conveyed and works relentlessly to decipher the code. He succeeds; the message, coming from another prisoner like himself, is "Have courage. . . ."*

Beyond this very limited universe of human contact,

* Arthur Koestler, who had been a political prisoner himself, relates a similar incident in *Darkness at Noon.*

there is of course the limitless world of escapism. Sleep, madness, suicide, these are the alternatives Kassner considers. The only possible means of suicide, he finds, would be to open a vein with his finger nail; he has none long or sharp enough. Although at one point, a Nazi guard tosses in a length of rope with the words "Work. Unravel," it is insufficient for hanging himself. To set about unraveling it would surely lead to madness, and the loss of sanity is what he now dreads as much as torture. Not madness per se, which would be a tenable escape mechanism, but the fear that in his madness he might give out information and violate his comrades' trust. Virtually unable to sleep, Kassner spends his days in prison in a state of semi-mad delirium. He starts by fantasizing that his wife Anna, now in Prague, is dead. He plays the childish game, "If I can count to 100 before the guard walks by, she's alive. . . ." only to realize that this in itself is a form of folly. He seizes on musical themes imbedded in his memory.

To stem the tide of mental disorder, Kassner makes a sustained effort to organize these elements into a coherent pattern. At one point he also undertakes a review of his life as a communist; he imagines himself speaking at a rally where he narrates his story to his comrades. Malraux is playing here on the theme of art as salvation. Where there is disorder and chaos, it is the function of the artist to impose order and form; Kassner, mentally shaping the narrative of his own life, assumes the surrogate role of writer. This simultaneously helps save his sanity and preserves his self-identity. The identity theme is further resolved, and ties this small tale rather melodramatically together, when Kassner learns that one of his comrades has just surrendered to the Nazis, identifying himself as Kassner. The real Kassner is thereby released from prison.

Somehow, a plane belonging to the underground communist movement, awaits him with a pilot who will fly him to freedom in Prague. In an episode recalling Malraux's recent flight over the desert, the two men brave an icy storm and succeed in reaching their destination in this primitive aircraft. Facile as the resolution may be, Malraux's study of near madness under prison conditions is powerfully rendered. The final pages, unfortunately, tend to diffuse the essential impact of *Le Temps du mépris.*

Kassner, joyously delirious from renewed contact with everyday reality—shops, wares, animals, people—finds his way to his apartment but his wife is not there. He goes off to an anti-fascist rally with little hope of finding her, yet feels a sense of "communion" with her, as he does with the vast crowd. In the scene where Kassner returns home and does find his wife and child, Malraux is clearly ill at ease in his effort to render such emotions and convey a scene of domesticity. All that is credible here is Kassner's realization, and Anna's, that their life will continue to be marked by separations since he is dedicated to a life of danger.

Le Temps du mépris had a poor critical reception; it was attacked both as propagandist and as artistically weak. Malraux subsequently agreed with the critical consensus concerning its literary merit, and virtually disowned the book, but he held to his statement in the preface that while *Le Temps du mépris* is infused with "passion," he had no "will to prove" anything. The work was intended as a tribute, and dedicated to certain German comrades for "what they endured and what they upheld." Hastily written no doubt, even more hastily than Malraux generally tended to write, *Le Temps du mépris* also seems to suffer from its imposed simplicity. Malraux craved a larger canvas and the freedom of broader brush strokes. That canvas he would shortly find on the battleground of Spain.

Le Temps du mépris appeared in London under the title *Days of Contempt*, less "poetic" but more accurate than *Days of Wrath*, for "*mépris*" infers something other than god-like ire or anger; it is an indictment of the disdain and contempt in which men sometimes hold the lives of other men. This had already been a key theme in Malraux's earlier fiction where Hong, Tchen, Kyo and others resist nothing so much as humiliation and subjugation; they seek the simple dignity of being a man and the respect of their fellow man. Malraux recognized in fascism that very contempt for free men. The verbless title—and all of Malraux's titles, surprisingly, are static and verbless—thus gives rise to a double-edged interpretation, suggesting the time has come for men to show *their* disdain for such contemptuous leadership and to overthrow their oppressors.

The phrase "*temps du mépris*" appears just once in this short narrative. Kassner is recalling a festival of youth in post-revolutionary Moscow, celebrated by a parade of 300,000 young Russians marching far into the night. Since they are all under twenty, he thinks to himself that not one of them could have known the "era of contempt" under czarism. The communist Kassner believed that with the downfall of the czarist regime, a new day for mankind had come, a time of freedom and peace. This is of course a pipe dream, a momentary distraction from his actual situation as a condemned man in a Nazi prison. From the standpoint of subsequent history, the irony is still more fierce.

As Malraux was writing, in 1935, Stalin was preparing mock trials to purge his opposition. Within a few years, the opportunistic Russian dictator would sign a nonaggression treaty with Germany, only to see his country invaded by Hitler. The Nazis simultaneously were initiating the most systematic slaughter of human beings the world had seen. Still closer in time, just a few months after Malraux's anti-Nazi novel was published, a new military dictator would emerge to destroy Spain's aspirations for a republic. As Malraux sensed, without knowing the sweeping extent of it, a new era of contempt for free men was upon us. Not really pro-communist but rather anti-fascist, *Le Temps du mépris* served the much needed function of propaganda at a time when Nazism had as yet inspired too little widespread alarm.

Malraux's response to the impending threat was to sound, more resonantly than ever, the clarion call of brotherhood. While he continued to be wary of marxist doctrine, and warier still of Soviet policy, Malraux did find in the communism of the 1920s and 1930s, the only coherent expression of man's faith in man as a working example of collective action. In tracing the progression of his thought, we find the key concept of "fraternity" growing stronger and stronger in each new novel, and as that idea gains force, the role of individualism and conquest diminishes. What critics have generally failed to underscore is that in Malraux's early novels, conquest and individualism are very closely linked to a particular moral cancer: *érotisme.*

In order to understand Malraux's thinking, one must distinguish between his use of *érotisme* and the English word, eroticism. Rather than connoting physical sensuality, *érotisme* implies the intellectualizing of sex. The "*érotique*" is one who cerebrates and calculates with the goal of manipulating—and thereby controlling—a sexual relationship. A celebrated example of *érotisme* is the eighteenth-century novel, *Les Liaisons Dangereuses*, by Choderlos de Laclos, where the principal characters dispassionately plot their sexual conquests. This, more than physical pleasure, provides their gratification. Malraux's interest in *érotisme* is not only evidenced by an article he wrote on Laclos, it is a persistent presence pervading the moral atmosphere in *La Voie royale*, continuing to a lesser extent in *Les Conquérants* and *La Condition humaine.*

When Claude first meets Perken on shipboard, he senses in the older man a certain "obsession" which is gradually revealed as *érotisme.* Neither lust, nor sadism, nor perversion, in any of the customary definitions of those terms, Perken's obsessional eroticism is a psychological corollary to his obsession with conquest. He has never fully found satisfaction in sleeping with a woman because he identifies sex with domination, and he cannot truly dominate unless he can simultaneously experience the feelings of his sexual partner. This being manifestly impossible, Perken suffers alienation and estrangement in the very act that should normally produce gratification. To master a woman physically should be a "conquest," but full mastery escapes Perken, so that in Malraux's metaphorical equation, conquest equals defeat.

In this light, Grabot is Perken's double: what Perken might have become had he been even more totally obsessed. Grabot's particular aberration is the desire to be bound nude by a woman in a dark room; nothing more. Such a fantasy is the symbolic opposite of his drive to dominate and conquer, to become a great "chief." Pushing his ironic proposition to its limits, Malraux has Grabot reduced to slave status, blinded, and bound to a treadmill in a jungle hut: the "conqueror" conquered by his own contradictory demons. At the moment when Claude and Perken discover him, we hear the cry of a peacock, ironically proud and fierce.

As a European in the orient, Malraux had noted that eroticism seems particularly aggravated when men find themselves in an alien culture, and that it reached an acute stage among colonials. In one of his very earliest writings, a comparative study of the morals, customs, and temperaments of east and west, Malraux had already raised the tantalizing question of sexual alienation, man's desire to know woman's experience, and the need to distinguish between loving and merely using a woman's body. That woman should remain a "stranger" haunted the young Malraux.

What Malraux's early heroes seem to fear most is humiliation, the loss of their dignity as men. Not being able to experience the other's sexual pleasure, as Perken seeks vainly to do, is psychologically tantamount to physical impotence. Garine, in *Les Conquérants*, makes a conscious effort to resist the debilitating obsession of *érotisme*. He seeks liberation by having sex with two native women at one time, as though the experience would be doubly liberating. Instead, like Perken, he finds only alienation and isolation.

Death, danger, and sexuality are curiously intermingled in *La Condition humaine*, when the young terrorist Tchen is asked how it felt to kill for the first time. "Proud," he replies. "Of being a man?" "Of not being a woman." Having murdered, he is no longer, in Malraux's lexicon, "a virgin." The murder scene itself incorporates the basic elements of Malrucian *érotisme*. The scene is a bedroom. As Tchen is about to strike (penetrate another's flesh with his knife), he becomes obsessed with the desire to know how it would feel to have that knife enter his own flesh. After stabbing the body to death—his "conquest"—Tchen feels alienation.

There is also another episode in *La Condition humaine* where the phenomenon of *érotisme* is brought into sharp relief. Ferral, a French financier in Shanghai, is driven wild that he cannot experience his sexual partner's physical and emotional sensations. In a moment of domineering rage, he insists on having sex with his mistress Valérie in a fully lighted room, as though watching her reactions would enable him to be more fully master of their copulation. When she refuses to forgive him for this, in fact jilts him, the furious Ferral remembers that he had promised to buy her a pet bird. In a scene of nightmarish proportions, he purchases a huge selection of birds and parrots (plus one kangaroo!) and releases them frantically in her room, all the while flicking off and on the light switch, as in a state of perverse sublimation. He then goes out and sleeps with a Chinese whore.

In their game of adversaries, Ferral thoroughly believes that man's possessing and woman's submitting is the only relationship two beings can have. Valérie more subtly observes: "Don't you realize, my dear, that women rarely 'submit' and that men never really 'possess' anything?" Ferral, trying mentally to project what a woman feels while being "possessed" by him, finally concludes that one only actually has sex with—only ever really possesses—oneself. The humiliating irony is that it happens in the presence of the adversary. The fact that this "captain of industry" is also suffering business losses at the time of his sexual setbacks seems symbolic of the doomed and spiritually bankrupt "chief."

Neither love nor sex ever played a significant role in Malraux's novels, but the solitary spectre of *érotisme*, a morbid expression of individualism, hovers uneasily over his early work. It is clear that Malraux, in his first three novels, was struggling with a psychological and moral problem, but also, on a larger scale, with a metaphysical and political problem. Although he found individualism ambivalently attractive, he realized that the will to conquest and power bears twin seeds of destruction. It is immanently tyrannical and threatening to the social order; its also breeds despair, alienation, and ultimately self-destruction. As Malraux proposed in the preface of *Le Temps du mépris*, the time had come for man to cease cultivating his individuality and recognize his fundamental communion with all men. *Le Temps du mépris*, set within a confrontation between communism and fascism, is a celebration of solidarity over solitude. As the spirit of fraternity moves increasingly to the fore of Malraux's thought, the demon *érotisme* is exorcised.

Much later on, writing at age 65, Malraux briefly resurrects the demon. Describing his World War II experiences, he admits that firing on the enemy produces a feeling akin to sexual sensation. And when the older Malraux recounts his dangerous flight over Sheba, he again uses sexual imagery to describe his reactions—and we recall that the legendary Queen of Sheba was a tempting beauty whom men sought in vain to conquer. Yet in *Le Temps du mépris*, he had already effected an artistic metamorphosis, transforming that "*farfelu*" desert flight into Kassner's symbolic flight to freedom: the return to homeland, family, and fellow man. He seems to be bidding farewell, perhaps reluctantly, to the daredevil in himself, and saluting a new self purged of demons. *Ave atque vale.*

6

False Dawn

Malraux had promised, on leaving Indochina, to continue to work for the independence movement that he had championed as an editor there. Except in conversations and speeches perhaps, there is little evidence of his having done so. His attention quickly turned to the revolutionary events in China, and with *Le Temps du mépris*, back in Europe. In 1933, he did publish one hard-hitting anti-colonial article, "S.O.S.," and in 1935, he contributed the preface to a book whose title seems to derive from that article: *Indochina S.O.S.* His interest in the east, however, had been eclipsed by an intense personal concern with impending European war.

When Italy invaded Ethiopia in the Fall of 1935, Malraux promptly appeared at the Mutualité and other public forums to denounce Mussolini's imperialism and the hypocrisy of calling it a "civilizing mission," which some of his fellow writers accepted. His efforts were in vain. In vain, too, the tragic soliloquy of Emperor Haile Selassie before a mute and paralyzed League of Nations. There was a madness in the air that would soon identity itself as World War II, and the dress rehearsal for that enormous spectacle was on the battleground of Spain.

In a swift, dizzying succession of events, during the early months of 1936, the Spanish people had elected a "popular front" government, representing a spectrum of political parties, then witnessed the rebellion of right-wing army generals who invaded the mainland from their base in Morocco, soon to be supported by tanks and planes furnished by Mussolini and Hitler.

Because of its political complexity, and also due to questions of terminology, the Spanish Civil War has been widely misunderstood, remaining to this day a subject of stormy controversy. Political uprisings are frequently staged by liberty-seeking factions opposing a conservative establishment, as in the French, American, and Russian revolutions, and again in the war-torn China of Malraux's novels. In Spain of the 1930s, these historical roles were reversed. The "Insurgents," led by Generalissimo Franco and his Falangist party, represented the political far right in revolt against a legitimately elected government they felt too dangerously "liberal." World opinion, then and still, has been sharply divided. When the catholic church declared for Franco, churches were burned. This, together with aid from communist Russia—however hesitant and belated, as Malraux would continue to stress—made the republican Loyalists appear to many as forces of barbarism, bolshevism, and anarchy. But the presence of Italian and German military power could only underscore Franco's alliance with fascism, further evidenced by his subsequent repression of liberties after victory. (Had Franco lost, would Spain have gone communist? The question continues to tantalize.)

In 1936, most men of good will were making a simple dichotomy with which few men of good sense could quarrel: the rights of the Spanish people had been violated; to side with Franco was to side with Hitler. One dramatic instance of intellectual dilemma was that of writer-philosopher Miguel de Unamuno, who first denounced the anti-clerical outrages of some Loyalists, but then, according to biographers, did an about-face on hearing cries of "Long live Death" at a fascist rally, and publicly repudiated Franco. Increasingly, Spain could be seen as the "first battle" of world war II, the dreaded but inevitable confrontation between free peoples and the fascist dictatorships.

While Nazi tank divisions and Italian aircraft poured into Spain, so too did substantial numbers of individual volunteers from uncommitted nations. Among them were British writers Stephen Spender and George Orwell, Hungarian-born Arthur Koestler, and, among less celebrated Frenchmen, André Malraux. Malraux's sudden appearance on the Spanish front, within a few days of the Falangist invasion in mid-July, was in some ways as foolhardy and "*farfelu*" as his Cambodian and Arabian escapades.

With no extensive knowledge of aircraft or piloting, Malraux sensed that what the Spanish loyalists needed was air power, and set about building up an international flight squadron under his command. Since France was neutral, he had to rely on his contacts and his ingenuity to get the needed planes. Before leaving Spain, only about six months later, he had succeeded in imposing organization upon chaos by establishing an effective air wing. His reason for leaving, moreover, was a self-appointed mission to America seeking support for the Loyalists. During this same period, he had also somehow found the time to draft his most ambitious novel, *L'Espoir*, published in late 1937 while the war still raged.

L'Espoir is a work of epic proportions that attempts to record the chaos of a particularly chaotic war. It is part documentary, part poem: panoramic in its visual sweep, yet with the intellectual calm and rigor of a philosophical dialogue. While a great deal happens to a great many characters, there is no "plot" in the conventional literary sense, and no "hero." Malraux's technique has rightly been called cinematic, full of quick cuts and dissolves designed to suggest either time lapse or simultaneity. Kaleidoscopic might perhaps be a better term, for the reader is never conscious of an omnipotent novelist staging a series of scenes; it is as though an invisible hand kept rotating the kaleidoscope lens, causing new configurations to fall into place.

In *For Whom the Bell Tolls*, published in 1940, Ernest Hemingway wrote of this same Spanish Civil War and chose to focus primarily on a single protagonist, Robert Jordan, and a single action, his blowing up a bridge. Malraux's optic is as diffuse as Hemingway's is concentrated. In a larger sense, however, their theme is the same. "No man is an island," begins the John Donne poem from which Hemingway derived his title. Malraux too was writing to dramatize the communal nature of man's lot and the need to establish our universal sense of brotherhood. The coherence of *L'Espoir* relies largely on this thematic unity since the sequence of events it depicts has no more pattern than the random unpredictability of war itself.

The opening chapter dramatizes the confusion that reigns right after Franco's surprise blitz, as the Loyalists attempt to organize their resistance. Against the rumble of trucks carrying rifles through the Madrid summer night (recalling the tense atmosphere of Shanghai in *La Condition humaine*), two Loyalist officers, Manuel and Ramos, are telephoning various railway stations along the line to the city in an effort to determine the location and movement of Insurgent troops. They identify themselves: "Workers' Committee Madrid." One reply, "Go screw yourself, bastard. Long live Christ the King!" clearly means that the station contacted has fallen to the Insurgents. Touch and go, on through the night, some stations have fallen, others have held. It is essential that Manuel and Ramos, like their counterparts throughout Spain, establish patterns of information, communication, and organization without which there can be no victory.

For the moment, the only unity is a sense of brotherhood in combat that permeates the air: ". . . taps on shoulders, fists raised and cries of 'salud!': the night was all fraternity." Later, as Manuel drives an old jalopy through the darkness, he feels "a vague unbounded hope wherein each and every man had something to accomplish on this earth." From start to finish, the word "fraternity" dominates *L'Espoir*, and it is so closely identified with the word "hope" of the title that the two become virtually synonymous. But Manuel and his comrades soon learn that hope and brotherhood alone will not stop tanks and planes.

The Loyalists face a two-fold problem: not enough weapons, planes, and equipment, and men too inexperienced to handle what little they have. The volunteer fighters are all fired with patriotic passion and enthusiasm, but lack discipline and training. Two scenes, early in the novel, underscore the need for arms and organization. Under enemy fire, a team of fifty Loyalists attempt to storm an army barracks by wielding a huge battering ram to break down the doors. In an era of mechanized warfare, it is like a scene from the Middle Ages. Nor do these apprentice soldiers invariably understand the need for unison action. A colonel named Ximénès is leading the attack on a small Insurgent stronghold in a cluster of farm houses. As the enemy is about to give in, some of his men—suddenly, and without orders—rush forth recklessly to do battle, each on his own. "Bravery is as worthless as fear," says Ximénès. One of Malraux's chief concerns in *L'Espoir* is to trace the transformation of uncoordinated bands of Spaniards and volunteer recruits from abroad into something resembling a fighting force, a unified corps that will give structure to the inchoate spirit of fraternity.

As in his previous novels, Malraux continues to be interested in why men fight, why they will risk their lives for a dream or an ideal. Like *Les Conquérants* and *La Condition humaine*, *L'Espoir* is a pseudo-documentary laced with philosophical dialogue, and like those earlier works, it is also a gallery of portraits. Although Malraux follows the events of the first eight months in Spain with relative fidelity, *L'Espoir* is less the chronicle of a war than a chronicle of men at war.

Out of his ever-growing concern with the relationship between the individual and the collective, there emerges a new theme: what it takes to become a leader of men. In this sense, *L'Espoir* may be read on one level as the account of Manuel's coming of age as a leader. Manuel is not the "hero" of the novel; Malraux persistently debunks heroics. He is not the protagonist; he shares the stage with a dozen characters. Yet Manuel, although we follow his career only intermittently, is the one figure who evolves from the first to the last scene of *L'Espoir*.

Unlike Kassner, in *Le Temps du mépris*, who is a dedicated communist party worker, Manuel is a "communist" without conviction. He belongs to the party simply because most members of his union belong. Young and easy-going, essentially apolitical, Manuel is a motion picture cameraman who is heading off on vacation just as war breaks out. Eager to serve his country, he finds himself assigned to command a group of volunteers. Over an eight-month span, Manuel will grow from his vague feeling of "fraternity" with his fellow soldiers to an intensive commitment and a hard-won responsibility. He is Shakespeare's Henry V leaving carefree pastimes behind as he assumes a mantle of leadership. In one scene, surprisingly like Henry's St. Crispin's Day speech, Manuel stands atop an old automobile to rally the spirits of his disgruntled and demoralized followers. With words, and with faith, he succeeds in reuniting them into an effective force; not so much by asking them to believe in him, but by assuring the men that he believes in them.

Throughout the series of crises and trials that mold Manuel, he has as his model and mentor a professional soldier, Colonel Ximénès, graying, sixtyish, partly deaf, called "Old Duck" by his troops, and, above all, a man who has mastered the art of inspiring confidence. Ximénès is a devout catholic who would normally have been serving with Franco's nationalist forces, but he is a passionate libertarian whose christianity finds its natural alliance with the Spanish people in their opposition to fascist oppression. Yet he knows the need for almost totalitarian discipline if wars are to be won. Attempting to train men with no experience in combat, he explains to them the importance of scattering and falling face-down to the ground in the event of air attack. Such an attack materializes even as he is speaking, but Ximénès does not give the order to disperse until the enemy planes are just overhead. After this initial experience of terror, the men are rid of their fears—and a better combat unit. In addition, Manuel realizes, Ximénès has earned their respect and loyalty; as a group, they look to him for the orders that will assure their best performance and hopefully their well being. Ximénès knows how to inspire the genuine affection of his troops without "courting" them. It is a lesson that Manuel will try to emulate.

Manuel also learns an important lesson from another man much older than himself, the peasant Barca. In the early days of the war, Barca has been wounded, and Manuel visits him in the hospital. The sight of the maimed and dying, their anguished cries, unnerve the inexperienced Manuel. In simple, sober terms, the old man describes why he decided to take an active part in the war. In a phrase recalling *Le Temps du mépris*, Barca identifies Franco's Insurgents as a political party "contemptuous of men." "They wanted me to respect them," he says, "but they were not worthy of my respect." Borrowing from the slogan of the French revolution, Barca sees man aspiring not only to liberty and equality, but most of all to fraternity.

As the weeks and months pass, Manuel discovers that his men respond better to his leadership when he happens to appear among them unshaven, when his rather aristocratic "Roman" profile resembles more that of a mediterranean fisherman. Yet he is resolved to resist any efforts to win them over by being a "good guy." Manuel also deplores the excessive emotionalism that makes men hate one another. Seeing the words "Death to Fascism" scrawled on a wall, he can understand the motivating passion but he also can realize how far off lies the goal of true brotherhood. His hope is that hatred can be transcended and transformed.

With each successive promotion—Manuel moves quickly up the ranks to lieutenant colonel—he senses the distance that separates Manuel the officer from the young man he used to be. The change is dramatized in the words of his friend Ramos, a former anarchist turned communist: "In the old days, I liked people better." In this succinct statement, Malraux underscores one of the basic dilemmas of his novel, perhaps of his entire work. Anarchy or terrorism, by whatever name we choose to call untrammeled individualism, is a privileged state in terms of self-fulfillment, but with no goal and no direction beyond its own expression, it is futile and destructive, resulting in a brotherhood of chaos.

Ironically, party discipline, such as that of communism, brings with it a machine-like solidarity that is effective in terms of action but also brings with it a loss of humanity. Under the circumstances of modern revolution, however, neither Ramos nor Manuel nor Ximénès has any choice. The isolated "conqueror" brandishing his fists against the skies or bombing street cars in protest, is an antiquated concept; discipline and organization are called for, and at that point in history, only communism had contrived the necessary apparatus. It is for that reason that Malraux dwells on the anarchist/communist opposition in *L'Espoir.* In the early pages, two characters with roots in anarchist activity play major roles: Puig and Négus, both symbolic of the rampant individualism that must be tamed if the war is to be won. "You know how to fight," Ximénès tells them, "but not how to win battles."

Puig is foolhardy in the worst tradition of combat

bravery; wearing a bloody "turban" which is actually a head bandage from an earlier encounter, he dies at the wheel of a truck which he drives smack into an enemy emplacement, as though personal defiance could destroy whole batallions. Négus, a skilled technician in sabotage and what we now call "guerilla" warfare, prides himself on his prison record and his love for the proletariat. He is most at home in individual grenade or flame-thrower attacks, acts of violence and potential self-sacrifice. As in his previous novels, Malraux seems to nurture a certain affection for such "conquering heroes" while unmasking their futile bravura.

Colonel Hernandez suffers from the sin of overweening magnanimity, rooted in pride. Although a professional military man like Ximénès, he is given to the grand gesture, making too much a public show of his liberal humanitarianism. He wants to see good in all men, even the enemy, and wants them to see good in him; he generously offers to allow letters written by Franco's officers to pass through his lines. Hernandez is an idealist who tries to set an example. But "setting an example" is a dangerous manifestation of individualism that will eventually cost him his life.

The titles and sub-titles that Malraux gives the various sections of *L'Espoir* are designed to shape our interpretation of the text. The first section is called *L'Illusion lyrique*, wherein the "illusion" is the belief that personal expressions of courage and brotherhood will somehow bring victory. With bittersweet irony, Malraux debunks that legend, proving the contrary. *Etre et Faire* is a linguistic play on two verbs; in English, the gerunds *Being* and *Doing*. The anarchists, and individualists like Hernandez, want to *be* something, to establish their own identity by leaving a "scar on the map." Others, notably the communists, want to *do* something; they set as their immediate goal a feasible program of accomplishment: defeating Franco and the nationalists. In addition to being a paean to brotherhood, *L'Espoir* often reads like a Machiavellian handbook.

"Effecting the Apocalypse" is the most extraordinary and memorable of Malraux's sub-section headings, summing up in a metaphor the meaning, as he sees it, of both revolution in general and the Spanish Civil War in particular. Borrowing from the Bible, Malraux implies that we already face the destruction of the world as we have know it heretofore, but that the new reign of peace and justice will not be the work of God but forged by man himself. Consistent with his other theses, Malraux further maintains that only a collective, tightly disciplined mass can "organize" the Apocalypse.

Malraux's spokesman for this argument is an intellectual, Garcia, a pipe-smoking anthropologist now serving as an intelligence officer, who "likes to talk a lot" and has a "taste for defining things." Garcia is both theoretician and pragmatist. It is he who formulates Malraux's dichotomy of *Being* and *Doing*, and also develops the notion of an organized Apocalypse. But Garcia perceives the present situation as interim—somewhere between revolt and revolution. In studied cartesian terms, he defines revolution as "the result of an insurrection, carefully plotted and planned, given shape by military struggle, and capable of rapidly replacing what it has destroyed."

"We're not there yet," he adds.

Warmer and more endearing than Garcia is Lopez, a sculptor who sees the Spain of 1936 as a graveyard of tombstones from which men will create monumental statues to man. He is surprised when others salute him as a military officer; he still thinks of himself as a simple artisan. Also from the domain of the arts comes Scali, a middle-aged Italian art historian who serves as an air corps volunteer. When one of Mussolini's airmen is captured, Scali is assigned to interrogate him. The boy is an art student and, Scali realizes, except for the fortunes of politics and war, this cocky young fascist might be one of his own students, engaged in study and research with him. Scali is also sent to help an elderly Spanish art historian, Alvear, to evacuate before the nationalist troops arrive. Alvear chooses to stay on. Without his books and paintings, the things to which he has devoted his life, his life would no longer have meaning. He is reminiscent of old Gisors in *La Condition humaine*, retreating from the world of action into a circumscribed world of his own.

The "loner" in Malraux's work, whether anarchist, individualist, idealist, or escapist, chooses his independent destiny at his risk, and that choice is of no practical value to society. What Malraux seems to be restlessly seeking is a truly communal society—men sharing and working together—but free from the excesses inherent in self-expression as well as the restraints inherent in Soviet communism. This calls for leadership, not dictatorship. Along with Manuel and Ximénès, there is one other character in *L'Espoir* who shows the qualities of leadership: one who has respect for individuals, can inspire their confidence, unite them, and himself embody their collective aspirations.

He is Magnin, a Frenchman who heads up the international air squadron in Spain. No communist, he is the experienced director of a French aircraft corporation, who has volunteered his services in Spain. His men call him "boss," but Magnin's desire, as a "revolutionary socialist," is that these fighting men, like his factory workers in France, have an understanding of what they are doing, and why. The men he is given to command, however, are a motley crew; among them, a Russian in exile who believes in democracy but nurtures a nostalgia for his homeland, an Englishman who wears a blazer, a renegade Frenchman fond of bizarre unmilitary costumes, and a testy legionnaire-type mercenary who drunkenly resists all efforts at discipline. "What I've got here is not an air squadron," Magnin realizes, "it's a guerrilla force." Magnin (who seems to have no first name) faces the same problem as Manuel (whose last name is never given): how to impose order and organization without undue constraint. This, in opposition to Perken's words in *La Voie royale*: "Constraint, that's what life is all about."

In the final pages of *L'Espoir*, it is Magnin and Manuel who hold the stage. Magnin learns from a Spanish peasant that there are enemy planes hidden near his village. He leads a reconnaissance and destruction mission in which one plane becomes grounded on a mountain top. A rescue mission is improvised, with virtually the entire population of the village participating. The men, in relays, are seen descending the mountainside bearing stretchers. Magnin, sitting on his mule like an "equestrian statue," observes the scene from two perspectives. First, at a distance, he sees only the vast snow-capped mountain with the peasants as tiny black specks against the white. As the procession nears—a great parade of fraternal humanity—he recognizes each of his men, and observes at closer range the faces of the peasants. The women, some with tears in their eyes, offer the wounded a taste of soup; they have used the last chicken in the village to make that soup. One old woman holds out a fragile china cup, perhaps her most priceless possession. These people, in their spirit of silent self-sacrifice, are a tangible expression of the brotherhood and solidarity that had filled the air when the war first broke out.

The scene is starkly overwhelming, so much so that readers and critics tend not to note another significant symbol in the same chapter. As he watches the peasants come down the mountain, and again as they pass, Magnin's attention is caught by the only other living thing in sight: an apple tree standing in the hard, stone-like earth, surrounded by a ring of dead apples rotting slowly back into the ground to reproduce themselves. Beyond the world of men, he becomes aware, there is the eternally rhythmic life-and-death cycle of renewal and vitality in nature. Malraux, customarily indifferent to both nature and symbolism, had found a symbol to which he would return.

L'Espoir ends, as the title indicates, on a more concrete note of hope: a major Loyalist military victory in which Manuel and his men have played a key role. Manuel, alone in the night, hears the sound of water rippling on stones, and the sound of piano music. He reflects on the rapid transformation of his life; Ximénès once told him he was "born for war." But we are re-born, as well . . . and Manuel wonders who he will become when peace returns. Thinking about that Spain of tomorrow, he also reflects on the infinite and wondrous possibilities of man.

Despite Malraux's statement that he had no "will to prove" in writing *Le Temps du mépris*, both that work and *L'Espoir* were intended, at least in part, to arouse the reader's indignation against injustice. *L'Espoir*, however, far surpasses its predecessor in artistic achievement. Some consider it Malraux's masterpiece. In order for the novel to have its impact, Malraux rushed it into print while there were still high hopes for the Loyalists. It is difficult to say whether he truly believed they could win in the long run. In March 1939, two years after the battle with which Malraux ends *L'Espoir*, Franco triumphed.

It may be that Malraux's "hope" was simply intended to encompass Manuel's patient faith: "One day there will be peace." Malraux had seen enough of blood, terror, and death, to realize that peace would be hard-won, and that devastation would inevitably precede the "apocalypse." In that same year, 1937, Jean Giraudoux wrote a modern version of the Greek tragedy *Electra.* In her relentless pursuit of justice, Electra has wrought destruction and death; the city is in flames. Seeing the sky as though on fire, one of Giraudoux's characters paradoxically states: "That is what is called dawn."

7

Quest for the Absolute

It was in the spring of 1937 that Malraux made his propaganda and fund-raising tour of the United States to aid the Spanish Loyalists. Armed with little English, Malraux was nonetheless received enthusiastically in the intellectual and leftist circles of Hollywood and New York. Just as in his homeland, this dark stranger was as much a legend as a prize-winning novelist. He wore the halo of a conquering hero fresh from battles in distant lands where his fellow fighting men were "real" communists. Yet he wore impeccable pinstripe suits, and his talk wandered freely and authoritatively over such disparate realms as art, revolution, cinema, politics, philosophy, and war. Even Americans who knew his novels only by hearsay flocked to meet him at cocktail parties or attend his lectures at Princeton and Berkeley.

Malraux's companion on this trip was an attractive and spirited brunette named Josette Clotis. His fifteen-year marriage with Clara had altogether dissolved at this point. He did not divorce her until after the war, however, feeling that if Clara, a Jew of German origin, fell into the hands of the Nazis, she might benefit from the protection of his name. Josette, like Clara, was a writer he had met through colleagues at the NRF; she would remain his mistress until her untimely death in a train accident towards the end of the war in 1944.

Returning from America, the couple settled briefly in

Paris, attending to the publication of *L'Espoir.* By the summer of 1938, they were once again in Barcelona where Malraux spent the next six months producing a film based to some extent on his novel. Although fascinated by the new medium of cinema since he was a teen-ager, Malraux had no technical knowledge or experience in film production. It was typical of his brash confidence and enthusiasm that he should undertake command of a flight squadron with virtually no flying experience, and then proceed to film the war in which he had fought with no practical knowledge of film technique. He was reversing roles with Manuel, his fictional movie cameraman who had become an army officer.

Malraux did create a sketchy scenario and script outline, but the film was consciously a work of improvisation. Following the vagaries of both the weather and enemy bombing attacks, Malraux and his crew set out to capture in documentary style the day-to-day presence of war. He wisely resisted any effort to recreate the novel in its sweeping scope, and there is no sustained focus on any central character such as Manuel or Magnin. The best scene—understandably, since it is so eminently visual in the novel—is the panoramic descent from the mountain, which has been hailed as one of the finest achievements ever of black-and-white cinematography.

By the time shooting was completed in January, 1939, Franco was victorious and the idea of "hope" was a fading illusion, not only in Spain but all throughout Europe. In rapid succession, Poland, Denmark, Norway, Belgium, and Holland were conquered by Hitler. France was soon to follow.

Not long before the start of world war II, Malraux and Josette Clotis had taken up summer residence in a southwestern region of France called Dordogne, where he wanted to work on a book dealing with "the psychology of art." With the outbreak of war, Malraux tried to enlist in the air corps; ironically, and despite his experience in

Spain, he ended up as a private in the tank corps, where his father had served in world war I. In the spring of 1940, without having seen combat, Malraux's unit was captured. On June 18, when General Charles De Gaulle, from his exile in London, proclaimed himself leader of the "Free French," Malraux was in a German army prison camp, not far from Paris in the medieval cathedral town of Sens, starting to write what would be his sixth and last novel.

After a few months he escaped, however, and by December found his way to relative safety on the Riviera where he was joined by Josette and the infant son to whom she had recently given birth, Pierre-Gauthier Malraux. Although he continued to work on his new novel, drafted sections of the book on art, and even sketched out a biographical study of Lawrence of Arabia, Malraux felt a growing uneasiness about his personal situation as a notoriously outspoken anti-fascist in Nazi-controlled Vichy France, and also a restless desire to participate in his country's liberation. When his efforts to contact the De Gaulle government in England, offering his combat services, failed, Malraux went "underground." In the Fall of 1942, leaving Josette and the baby in her family's care, he left the Riviera and began actively seeking to join one of the resistance movements that were organizing in Dordogne and Périgord.

By the Spring of 1944, shortly after Josette had borne his second son Vincent, the extraordinary Malraux had become "Colonel Berger," an officer of the French Resistance whose exploits added a new chapter to his personal legend. Much as he had done in Spain, Malraux recruited a body of men under his command by promising to supply them with arms, parachutes, and other combat equipment—and somehow keeping that promise.

According to his own account, written twenty years later, Malraux was captured by the Germans again, and this time put before a firing squad. Just before the fatal moment, however, he was recalled for additional interrogation. Suspiciously paralleling his novel *Le Temps du mépris*, it was a case of mistaken identity that saved his life. His half-brother Roland was for some reason being sought by the Nazis, and André did not fit the description. To add to the melodramatic confusion, as Malraux points out, his correct name was *Georges*-André Malraux. Before the matter could be resolved, the Germans were fleeing the U.S. and allied forces, and Malraux took his brigade to the Alsace-Lorraine area where the final battles of the war would be waged.

There, just before the armistice, "Colonel Berger" Malraux met General De Gaulle, who would later adopt him as propaganda chief in his post-war political "revolution." It was *Les Conquérants* all over again. Some critics have stressed the extensive use Malraux made of his personal adventures in writing his novels. More astute critics, including Malraux himself, note the degree to which his fiction often seemed to foreshadow the events of his life.

Malraux never wrote what might be called a "world war II novel." *Les Noyers de l'Altenburg* (The Walnut Trees of Altenburg), begun in a prison camp in 1940, published in 1943 in neutral Switzerland, is a very different kind of novel from his others in tone, style, and structure. Yet he continues to pursue his persistent quest for a definition of man. As its very title suggests, this is a serene and contemplative work. Action, for the first time, is subordinate to thought, and *Les Noyers de l'Altenburg* reads like an essay on death as much as a novel. Is it a novel at all? The unorthodox structure—a memoir within a memoir—puzzled many readers and critics. Malraux had frequently been accused of sketchy composition, ellipsis, chronological fuzziness, and a disregard for form. In *Les Noyers de l'Altenburg*, he attempted his most complex fictional narrative, but also perhaps his most skillfully ordered and unified.

The premise is actually a simple one, a variation on the eighteenth-century device wherein the author announces that he has discovered the manuscript of someone's memoirs, which in turn constitutes the substance of the novel. In this instance, a young world war II soldier named Berger tells us that he is going to write the memoirs of his father, Vincent Berger, who had jotted down notes on his "encounters with man," but never assembled them into book form before his death in world war I.

Whether this is ultimately the father's story or the son's—or a telescoping of the two—remains problematical. A curious kind of unity-in-duality is further provided by the fact that Bergers are Alsatian. Since Alsace-Lorraine was perpetually disputed territory, fate dictated that Vincent Berger fought with the Germans while his son, a generation later, is fighting against the Gemans. The name Berger, which Malraux would later adopt as his pseudonym in the French underground resistance, can be either German or French, according to pronunciation. One notes, too, that "berger" in French means "shepherd," thereby conveying the idea of guide, pastor, or leader.

Just as Malraux himself was held prisoner at the twelfth-century cathedral at Sens (about fifty miles southeast of Paris), young Berger, wounded in the hip and captured by the Germans, is being held at the thirteenth-century cathedral at Chartres (about fifty miles southwest of Paris). Just as the roar of trucks carrying arms sets the stage for both *La Condition humaine* and *L'Espoir*, German tanks now rumble past, shaking the very cathedral. A familiar wartime confusion reigns: soldiers opening blood-caked tins of food, some writing letters, others staring blankly into space. Wounds are being dressed. There are rumors: Pétain arrested, armistice, Hitler has entered Paris, Pétain dead, a change of command, another country invaded. . . .

What interests the narrator most are the soldiers' letters, their attempts to keep in touch with family. These letters are to be censored of course, and must follow a formula: "I am well/wounded/ . . . well cared for/ . . . etc." The narrator knows the men's desire to write more than such platitudes, their urge to express some emotion or some small truth. He knows too that most of these letters will never even reach their destination. Yet the men doggedly write on, their words giving them hope. It is in that same spirit that young Berger, almost twenty-five years to the day after his father's death, begins the "memoirs" of Vincent Berger: "writing is the only way to keep alive."

The inner narrative opens with the death of Dietrich Berger's, the narrator's grandfather. Within a few days of Vincent's return from a lengthy foreign mission, Dietrich has committed suicide. Moved, if not outwardly, by his father's suicide, Vincent expresses his "respect" for a man's right to kill himself: "Whether suicide is an act of courage or not is a question that concerns only those who have not killed themselves."

A certain air of mystery hangs over the old man's death for he had only just told his son two days before, "whatever happens, if I had to live life over again, I would want none other than Dietrich Berger's." It is the phrase "whatever happens" that indicated premeditation perhaps. To compound the mystery, Dietrich has left a note reading, "My express wish is not to have a religious burial"—but he had then quite vigorously struck out the word "not."

This grandfather had always been an eccentric, a willful man, at odds with the church. He had once set off on foot for the Vatican to protest a change in Lenten rules, and had not since set foot in the local church. Instead, every Sunday, he would kneel outside the church, sometimes in the mud, holding an umbrella; even after growing deaf, he seemed to follow the service from memory. His suicide note was thus in keeping with his ambivalent feeling towards catholicism—or perhaps his last tragic "tease."

The only family member who is not present at Dietrich's funeral is his brother Walter, also a maverick and an enigma. Proud and strong-willed, he is a cripple who will only be photographed standing up, his crutches hidden under his long coat. He boasts that he was a close friend of Nietzsche, but the latter's correspondence with Walter reveals little warmth or even respect for him. A trained philosopher, Walter spends endless hours revising the table of contents of a giant book he is planning to write. His great concrete achievement has been to establish and preside over an annual colloquium, attended by the foremost European scholars and held in the former priory of Altenburg. It is there that Vincent Berger, a "man of action" just back from six years away from Europe, will test wits with intellectuals, but first comes a flashback recounting his career as a westerner in the near east.

A brilliant young philosophy professor, Vincent had given up his university post to join the German embassy in Turkey. In behalf of his government, he has worked to promote an alliance of Turkish nations, a kind of empire. As he becomes more passionately and personally involved, Berger is adopted by the leader of this "Young Turk" movement, Enver Pasha, as his chief aide. Eventually, however, he becomes disenchanted. He finds no real enthusiasm, no unified collective urge among the people themselves to forge such an alliance; it is only the dream of a small group of autocrats. After seven years, he returns home, there to face two dramatic events: the suicide of his father and an experience of self-revelation at the Altenburg Colloquium of his uncle.

Given Malraux's preoccupation with the legendary "Lawrence of Arabia," who participated in the struggle for pan-Arabic unity, critics often stress the analogy between the British hero and Malraux's fictional Berger. Another theory is that of a marxist critic who sees in Berger an indication of Malraux's growing disenchantment with the expansionist policies of communist Russia. While there may be an element of truth in this, one must necessarily note that there is a recurring dramatic structure in Malraux's novels: that of the adventurous foreigner joining in the conflicts of other countries, and that this, in turn, reflects his own personal experiences.

Berger, like Malraux himself and a number of his other fictional protagonists, is cast as an adventurer or fighting man who is also an intellectual. Also borrowed from experience, the model of the "Altenburg" colloquium is generally believed to be the annual conferences at Pontigny in which Malraux had participated. Not one given to auto-criticism, let alone self-mockery, Malraux seems at least to suggest in *Les Noyers de l'Altenburg* that intellectual colloquy and theoretical speculation on man may very well be "words, words, words. . . ." He seems to be looking beyond action and beyond theory for some form of transcendant expression that will respond to his quest for an understanding of man's fundamental meaning, his purpose and destiny, his very presence in the universe.

The topic of the philosophical colloquium is staggering in its immensity: The Permanence and Metamorphosis of Man. It was to have been The Eternal Elements of Art, but this was changed by Walter Berger after his brother Dietrich's death. Here a note of subtle satire enters. We are asked implicitly to accept that an abrupt change of topic is of no concern to the participants; the intellectual (the "professional" intellectual) will go on mouthing his "set piece," his pet ideas and cliché theories no matter what the subject under discussion may be.

Although it is perfectly normal for such a symposium to be held in a library, Malraux provides insistent reminders that the participants live in a "bookish" world. They sit surrounded not only by shelves of books but by works of art, sculptures and paintings, as well as photographs of Tolstoy and Nietzsche, and the death masks of Beethoven and Pascal. With pretentious unpretentiousness, Walter Berger is seated at a simple desk, one step higher than the others, and refers to the Altenburg priory as "just an old barn." One sentence in Malraux's description of the library seems paradoxical: "Darkness entered through a great stained-glass window." The window suggests the cathedrals that figure importantly throughout the novel; the idea of darkness "entering" suggests that no light may be shed here by the most brilliant minds of Europe.

One of the participants has spent a lifetime cultivating the manner of the esoteric symbolist poet Mallarmé, that of a Master expounding dogma to admiring disciples. Others affect the skepticism of Socrates and Montaigne, but in a theatrical way; they theorize endlessly and extemporaneously to prove that for all our centuries of accumulated civilization, we still know nothing of man's nature. They chatter on, invoking great names from Plato to Hegel, moving from dogma to doubt, from doubt to dogma. It is a "dialogue with culture," Vincent mentally notes, wherein an idea never stems from a fact, but rather from another idea, an infinite progression into abstraction.

This is a game they have been playing for years, one often marked by a form of charlatanism they call "the elephant trick." This is a violation of logic in which a set of terms under discussion—art and the beansprout as examples of metamorphosis—engender a nonpertinent term leading to digression: "Art and the beansprout, gentlemen, differ from the elephant in that the elephant is an animal of great size and weight, etc." The discussion is then open to the subject of elephants. As Malraux wryly remarks: "There had been no war in Europe for forty years."

Expressing disenchantment with sterile intellectuals

("A race apart"), Malraux penetrates the superficial sham of the colloquium by juxtaposing two divergent points of view. These are embodied in the fictional characters of Vincent Berger and a German anthropologist named Möllberg, who has returned from Africa with a wealth of research on tribal customs. He is expected at this very meeting to summarize his theory of man as the product of historical continuity. He does just the opposite.

Although Möllberg had gone to Africa persuaded that such a theory could be substantiated, that a comparative study of civilizations would yield the common denominator of "fundamental man," he has unearthed only a plurality of cultures, rooted in a variety of beliefs and behavior patterns. Convinced that any definition of "fundamental man" would be false, Möllberg has symbolically scattered the pages of his projected manuscript over the desert. The summation of his lengthy discourse at the Colloquium is a bleak and desperate statement:

"If mental structures can vanish without a trace like the dinosaur, if the cycles of centuries reveal only man in a bottomless void, if the human adventures persists only through relentless metamorphosis, it matters little that men bequeath their theories and their methods for a few brief centuries: for man is a creature of chance, and in the last analysis, the world is rooted in oblivion."

This is a view that neither Vincent Berger nor Malraux can subscribe to, or rather it is one that both the protagonist and his creator refuse to accept.

One of the participants points to two Gothic statues carved in walnut as proof of man's "continuity." Möllberg retorts that the statues are made from logs of wood, that there is no such thing as "fundamental walnut" any more than there is a concept that can be called "fundamental man." As the debate rages on, Vincent leaves the library and enters the woods surrounding the Altenburg priory. Moving through the darkness, he stops to contemplate two majestic walnut trees, towering against the twilight sky and framing the view of Strasbourg cathedral in the distance, "erect like a cripple at prayer."

A network of vines, rolling down the valley to the river, bear testimony to centuries of patient human endeavor and consciously continuous productivity. But most of all Berger is transfixed by the two giant walnut trees, rooted deep in the bowels of the earth, asserting their everlasting endurance in the skyward thrust of their boughs; he sees them as living wood, symbols of "endless metamorphosis." The scene distinctly recalls Magnin, in the closing pages of *L'Espoir*, standing by the apple tree in a similar moment of revelation. For Berger, Möllberg's theory is refuted by the walnut trees; a vision triumphs over the intellect, and the poetry of that vision, against all logic and reason, proclaims man's common destiny, his fundamental universal permanence.

Vincent's solitary illumination in a twilight wood is subsequently reconfirmed by his experience in the world of men. A year later, serving as an officer with the German army on the Russian front, he finds himself a passively protesting witness to the first poison gas attack. He watches the German foot soldiers move into Russian territory as the waves of lethal gas subside. Suddenly, he sees them returning, refusing to advance. They have thrown aside their weapons, but not in cowardly retreat; in a communal gesture of defiant compassion, each German is carrying a Russian soldier on his shoulders. A mission of terror has become a mission of mercy as these enlisted men, in revolt, demand ambulances and medical care for the enemy troops who have been gassed.

Inspired by their extraordinary action, Berger himself strides towards the Russian lines in search of a soldier to save: an action that will give his life final meaning. In a bluish haze of lingering gas, a moment of near-mystical, transcendant agony, Berger senses a profound revelation of human brotherhood. His earlier intuition of a fundamental quality in man—our innate and everlasting defiance of destiny—has proved manifest. Like his father, Dietrich Berger, Vincent can affirm that given a life to live over again, he would choose his own.

It is again 1940, the Chartres cathedral, and Vincent's son concludes his father's "memoirs" with a comparable affirmation of faith. Just before their capture, he and three fellow soldiers had been trapped when their tank fell into a ditch, the target of German bombardment. Out of an endless night of darkness and fear, they escape into the morning light. Cold water from a pump, the sight of barnyard animals in the sun, even a spider web gleaming with dew, all seem like miracles. The world takes on a pristine quality, as in Rimbaud's great prose poem, *Après le déluge* (After the flood). "It was thus," writes Berger/Malraux, "that God perhaps gazed upon the first man."

His revelation, a hymn to life on the theme of resurrection, is spoken with the awe of an explorer discovering a new world. Malraux's last "conqueror" has triumphed over anguish and solitude. Like the walnut trees at sundown, the countryside at dawn bears witness to the perennial rebirth of the universe and the cyclical transcendance of man, both miracles of metamorphosis and continuity.

Malraux dedicated *Les Noyers de l'Altenburg* to his new-born son, and went off to war again.

8

View from Olympus

Although he will almost surely be best remembered as a novelist, André Malraux wrote no fiction during the last thirty-three years of his life. The promised sequels to *Les Noyers de l'Altenburg*, published in 1943, never appeared. He seems to have felt that the traditional novel form had largely exhausted its narrative possibilities; he was undoubtedly also aware that what he had achieved in *Les Noyers de l'Altenburg* was perhaps less a novel than a philosophical essay. His pen was not idle, however; during the early years of his feverish involvement with Gaullist politics, the protean Malraux began to launch a rather astonishing series of highly subjective essays on art and civilization.

In 1947, he created a great stir by publishing the first of three volumes to be called *La Psychologie de l'Art* (The Psychology of Art). By 1951, he had thoroughly reworked the random, rambling text of this art series and changed its over-all title to *Les Voix du Silence* (The Voices of Silence), a superbly printed single volume containing more than four hundred photographic reproductions, one of the most ambitious books on art ever attempted and one of the most widely discussed works of non-fiction of our times. Hailed in some quarters as a work of genius, it was attacked by certain members of the art establishment as presumptuous, pretentious, and inaccurate. Some critics found it spellbinding; others, incoherent and unintelligible. Edmund Wilson, reviewing the earlier version, judged Malraux's reflections on the psychology of art as constituting one of the most important works of the century. A deluxe American edition, priced at $25, appeared in time for Christmas, 1952, and was a popular gift item that year; considering the rigorous complexities of Malraux's thought, *The Voices of Silence* may still sit attractively inarticulate on many a suburban coffee table.

Over the next two decades, Malraux would continue to publish in this same vein: a three-volume series dealing with sculpture, statuary, and bas-reliefs throughout civilization: *Saturne*, a pictorial essay on Goya, and a four-volume work called *La Métamorphose des Dieux* (The Metamorphosis of the Gods). During that same period, the indefatigable Malraux was charged by his publisher, Gallimard, with editing two other major art books covering the complete paintings of Leonardo da Vinci and those of Vermeer de Delft.

If Malraux's sudden appearance on the scene of nationalist politics had been disconcerting, his emergence as art critic and historian proved equally controversial and unexpected. But only to those whose knowledge of his background and interests was incomplete. Far from being a newcomer to the world of art, he had been intensely involved since 1920. No sooner having established himself in Parisian publishing as a brash young spirit of nineteen, Malraux turned his attention and his innate critical talents to contemporary art. At that moment in time, Paris was not only a "melting pot" of international painters—Picasso, Gris, Modigliani, and dozens of others—it was a cauldron of experimentation in art. Poets Guillaume Apollinaire and Pierre Reverdy, themselves pursuing a bold new expression in the verbal domain, were attempting to define in critical terms the innovative esthetics of cubism. Although younger and less illustrious, Malraux attracted attention with the critical articles he contributed to the avant-garde reviews of the time. Whether writing on poetry or painting, Malraux showed exceptional insight and the ability to formulate his intuitions in altogether startling and unhackneyed terms. In these early essays, it is now easy to find the germs of the radical thinking that produced *Les Voix du Silence* twenty-five years later. Novelist and agnostic, Malraux resolutely maintained that from the very beginning his true "home" and his religion was art.

What makes *Les Voix du Silence* and its succeeding volumes so maddeningly difficult is perhaps less their overwhelming subject matter—the art of mankind throughout the centuries—than Malraux's apocalyptic and deliberately elliptical style. We are accustomed to reading art history within a chronological framework, but Malraux breaks down the barriers of time and civilization to confront us with unwonted comparisons of prehistoric and modern, Christian and pagan, eastern and western, art. Malraux takes the view from Olympus: one singularly well informed connoisseur surveying the output of the ages from the four corners of the earth. We are also given to expecting from our museum guides an exposition bathed in clarity and logic. But Malraux is not academically tracing historical developments, he is challenging us to re-think, in keeping with his highly intellectualized and revolutionary precepts, some very basic concepts: the meaning of art, the function of art, the origins of artistic creation, the relative relationship of esthetic styles across time and from one culture to the next.

For such an enterprise, the ABC's of conventional discourse will not suffice. In any case, Malraux had the most associative of minds, given to leaping from one idea to another. A word, a name, a thought frequently generates its like, its opposite, or both, and the reader often feels caught up in a maelstrom of prolixity as though riding a roller-coaster through a labyrinth of ideas. Malraux also had a prodigious memory, drawing examples and comparisons freely from the wealth of countless works of art that he had seen and studied during his world-wide travels over twenty-five years. In some ways, it would appear necessary to share Malraux's vast knowledge of art in order fully to appreciate the breadth and depth of *Les Voix du Silence*. Such is not altogether the case, however; the intelligent reader with a basic disposition for the plastic arts can, with patience and fortitude, find Malraux's unorthodox exposition both stimulating and rewarding.

What one *learns* in terms of names, dates, and facts, would not be a proper measure of that experience; but it would be difficult to emerge from a serious reading of *Les Voix du Silence* without finding one's personal approach to works of art appreciably altered. One of Malraux's basic innovative concepts is that of "*le musée imaginaire*." This was indeed the title of volume I of *La Psychologie de l'Art*, and "imaginary museum" has been quite felicitously translated into English as "museum without walls." Taking the olympian view of mankind back to its beginnings, from the moment when man first traced his image and his impressions on the walls of caves, Malraux astutely observes that the idea of a museum, a place to visit and to view works of art, is but two centuries old, an altogether "new" idea within the total history of civilized man. In our own time, that idea has again undergone a radical shift thanks to techniques of reproduction which makes copies of great paintings and sculpture available on a scale heretofore inconceivable. The convergence of printing and photography enables the masterpieces of the ages, once the province and often the property of the elite, to be viewed and assimilated by great masses of people.

At the same time, modern man has increasingly developed an eclectic and relativistic viewpoint on art. While we may still study "schools" of painters and "periods" of stylistic achievement, such temporal limitations have given way to a broader field of perception. We can now compare, side by side, the gods and the fetishes, the portraits, landscapes, and still lifes of one age with those of another. This comparative method simultaneously reveals how each civilization conceived of itself in visual terms, and how man—Malraux's fundamental man—asserts his incontestable constancy across historical time.

There is also a new-found measure of freedom if one accepts Malraux's persuasive argument. He points out, indeed underscores, the fact that the icon, the crucifix and kindred artifacts are now released from the "sacred" status for which they were originally created; once functionally objects of veneration, they now enjoy the autonomy of objects of art, to be considered with other comparable objects of art. As Malraux sees it, a medieval representation of the Virgin was, for its viewers, *the* Virgin. No longer historically subject to a medieval christian mystique, we perceive this same object today as the product of a creative act: the expression of a collective belief, of course, but also the expression in wood or stone, on glass or canvas, of an individual stylistic vision, that of its particular creator. This naturally leads Malraux to an essential interrogation: the psychology of artistic creation.

Contrary to accepted convention, Malraux does not see the artist as looking out on life or nature and seeking to reproduce that reality either "as it is" or "as he perceives it." Malraux advances the argument that just as a work of art is autonomous and an end unto itself, so art is created not so much as the perception of the object by the artist but between the artist and the works of art that are his cultural heritage. In other words, according to Malraux, the budding artist does not work in a void, choosing this or that object to portray; he rather starts by seeking to imitate the prevalent stylistics of his era and those immediately preceding—the inheritance of his fellow artists. Malraux challenges the occidental cliché that "art imitates nature" by counter-asserting that a given painter does not set out to reproduce an apple, a nude, or a mountain but first to duplicate an accepted esthetic model—and then, gradually, to repudiate that particular set of stylistics by forging his own original individual style. The challenge comes not from the apple, but from prior paintings of apples: the response is a new mode of conveying the quintessence of "appleness."

Malraux clearly sees the artist as promethean, a rebel who renounces the existing order, and thereby moves humanity one step forward in its self-perception and self-realization. Malraux's vocabulary, in developing this theme, is altogether revealing. In existential terms, he sees the artist as "wresting" meaning from the chaos and absurdity that constitute the dumb universe surrounding him. The creative act is a "conquest" over forces that might otherwise defeat or consume man without his innate ability to impose human will, human order, and human form on an unintelligible world. It is a vocabulary of struggle and triumph. To Malraux, art is not only an anti-history, it is an anti-destiny, and to return to the obsession of his novels, it is man's universal way of saying "no" to the void of death, for the artist as hero constitutes proof, from age to age, of the continuity of fundamental man.

This, of course, was the great question raised in *Les Noyers de l'Altenburg*: whether man may rationally be considered to have any such meaningful continuity, or whether civilizations simply rise and fall with no underlying connection and coherence. In that novel, Malraux's last, the hero Berger attempts to refute the pessimism of Möllberg, the anthropologist who staunchly asserts the meaningless of man, adrift in a cosmos without pattern. Words and logic, the traditional armature of western civilization, fail Berger who then finds his pattern and his symbol in the eternally cyclical walnut trees. Although they are in a sense manifestations of brute nature, the chaos and the absurdity of the universe, they are also potentially the mirror of man's meaning in that he can create saints out of walnut trees and thereby leave a lasting image for future generations and civilizations to come.

Möllberg is generally believed to be a fictional portrait of Leo Frobenius, a noted German archeologist and anthropologist of the early twentieth century. Recent critics have also pointed out that Möllberg's negativistic, defeatist viewpoint derives from Oswald Spengler's *The Decline of the West.* In that work, published in 1918 just at the end of world war I, Spengler argues not only that civilizations rise and fall without viable inter-continuity, but that our own western civilization has effectively spent itself and will give way to a new oriental dominance. *Les Noyers de l'Altenburg* may thus be seen as Malraux's attempted refutation of Spengler in symbolic terms, while *Les Voix du Silence* and Malraux's other books on art would be his effort to counter Spenglerian philosophy with a positive exposition, however unsystematic, of the case for fundamental man.*

It is interesting to note that British historian Arnold Toynbee, during the 1930's and 1940's, was also developing a philosophy of civilizations, systematically rooted in Hegelian dialectic. In his monumental *Study of History*, Toynbee advances a theory of "challenge and response" as evidence of historical continuity. Malraux's notion of the artist's "response"—two antithetical forces producing a new and forward-moving synthesis—may be seen as a parallel theorem, and also an indication that humanist

* One singularly tantalizing question remains unanswered. Over a fifty-year span, Malraux as writer and statesman observed a resurgence of oriental peoples and acknowledges that phenomenon with undisguised assent. While addressing Spengler's basic theory and calling for a renovation of western values, Malraux remained strangely silent on Spengler's corollary: the rise of the east as a threat.

intellectuals of the mid-twentieth century felt the need to assert themselves as adversaries to Spengler.

One attack on Malraux's theories might be that they center in too elite a fashion on a relatively rare phenomenon, the artist of genius whose vision and style leave an indelible trace throughout time. If, however, we read "artist" as a metaphor for *man*, Malraux's example reminds us of our basic potential for defiance, that part of the individual that says no to the absurd, no to subjection, humiliation, and tyranny, and in a transcendant sense, even no to death. Reduced to this premise, Malraux's extensive writings on art serve as a gloss to his novels and an echo to their plea, enabling us to hear again, through the chorus of the "voices of silence," Malraux's dauntless affirmation of man, rooted less in logic than in faith.

The uproar of antagonism in art circles that surrounded the publication of these bold essays was largely rooted in misinterpretation. Since he was formally untrained in the technical aspects of art history and art criticism, it seemed easy to attack Malraux's effrontery in tackling such a vast and privileged domain. What few realized at the time is that Malraux was essentially writing neither criticism nor history as such, but rather one man's view of man, that of an observer in an olympian reviewing stand, surveying the parade of civilizations. As art history or critical methodology, *Les Voix du Silence* may be faulted, but Malraux pretended to neither discipline; he was composing a philosophical poem in praise of man. And while Plato claims that poets fabricate and lie, we discover on reading poetry more intuitive truths, and deeper, than technicians or logicians can ever chart for us.

"Art and death are all I hope to discover here," wrote André Malraux in one of his late works. In essence, these forbidding presences seem all that he had ever sought to confront. The thrust of a lifetime of thought, action and reflection, centers on their very confrontation.

If we interpret "art as conquest" as an equation of man vs. destiny, it is clear that Malraux never for a moment swerved from his initial preoccupation with this fundamental struggle.

Gifted with daring that perhaps only an autodidact would venture, Malraux at twenty-five had already called for a total reevaluation of man's concept of man. His essay, "D'une jeunesse européenne" (On European Youth), and *La Tentation de l'Occident* (The Temptation of the West), a juxtaposition of eastern and western civilizational values, came only to attract really widespread attention years later, at the time when Malraux was established with his books on art as a "civilizationalist."

La Tentation de l'Occident is essentially a philosophical essay in epistolary form: an exchange of letters between a young Chinese named Ling who is visiting Europe and his French counterpart travelling in China, who signs himself simply "A.D.," suggesting "André." It is a fictitious situation, but the book has neither the flow and movement of a novel, nor is any effort made to give characterization to Ling or A.D. They are merely vehicles for the transmission of ideas in a book that reads rather like a debate on the future and the fate of civilization.

In one respect, *La Tentation de l'Occident* suggests those eighteenth-century works of Voltaire, Montesquieu, and others who popularly used the literary device of orientals visiting Paris as a means of satirizing French customs and politics. But Malraux's intention is far from satirical; he is setting forth a series of challenging propositions on matters social, political, and metaphysical that embrace virtually the whole of man's fundamental concerns—an ambitious, almost pretentious, project for an unknown writer of twenty-five.

A.D. represents the culmination of western individualism, the concept of man *versus* the universe, man striving to master his surroundings and his condition. As long as christianity prevailed, a certain harmony prevailed between man and his world. But A.D. subscribes to the Nietzschean tenet that God is dead. He also perceives the moral dilemma posed by Dostoyevsky's corollary: if God is dead, then everything is possible. But if everything is possible, then nothing is; man's life is chaos and void, and the very concept of man must be defined anew.

Ling, the product of a very different and even older civilization, views with misgiving European man's preoccupation with action as a mode of life and the cult of personality. By way of contrast with the idea of man being "separate" from the universe, Ling's oriental teaching has instilled in him the concept of harmony and attunement to the rhythmic cycles of life wherein man is one with the world and assimilated as part of its being.

The will to power and glory is alien, even repulsive, to him for it disrupts a natural order. Acceptance rather than defiance is the code instilled in him, and he finds the westerner's efforts to impose his own image on that of the world to be ludicrous, dangerous, and absurd. Even the European notion of sexuality, infused as it is with obscure demonic passions, he finds self-destructive. Ling's formulation of the oriental mystique, his analysis of the west's impassioned desperation as futile, and his rejection of the "real" and the rational pose a tempting alternative to the already skeptical A.D.

With his innate predilection for dialectic and paradox, Malraux makes no overt judgment on the validity of either Ling's or A.D.'s thoughts and reactions. The give-and-take of their respective arguments seems to hang in the balance. Today's reader, retrospectively aware of Malraux's fascination with the east, may unconsciously assume that he was downgrading western values in order to "preach" eastern philosophy, but a careful reading of the text belies this. One of Malraux's basic points, to which he returns in his art books, is that civilizations see themselves best, indeed discover themselves, through the thoughtful encounter with other civilizations. Ling and

A.D. are in the process not only of observing and absorbing an alien culture but on voyages of self-discovery.

It is true that both are quite harsh in their evaluation of European civilization, but this does not mean that Malraux was indiscriminately taking sides. His seemingly uncritical analysis of eastern ways ends in dilemma. When A.D. writes of his visit to a distinguished Chinese intellectual, Wong-Loh, it becomes apparent that the east is in a state of troubled crisis comparable to that of the west. According to Wong-Loh, who seems perhaps more Malraux's spokesman than either of the younger men, traditional oriental values are soon destined to crumble. Tempted by the west's achievement in the material domain, the east has begun to succumb to European ideas in all domains. The new breed of young Chinese wants to be an "individual" and is courting an unwonted form of self-expression that is indigenous to the cult of personality. Abandoning the balance of "man-in-the-world," he is dangerously pursuing alienation from the world, a state which has already produced the bankruptcy of western values.

Even the title, meaning simply "the temptation *of* the west," is equivocal. Is the west being tempted by the east—or is it the contrary? Both interpretations are gramatically possible. With bold lucidity, and an ever-present measure of irony, Malraux cut sharply through what is actually a dual dilemma, and which he was among the first to perceive. The contradictory impact of individualism and marxism on the Chinese mentality is one of the problems he set out to explore in *Les Conquérants*. Garine sees the Chinese as "jellyfish;" "We're the backbone!" he proclaims. But what, Malraux implies, if the "backbone" is broken?

Like A.D., Malraux himself was a young European, disenchanted with his heritage, looking to another civilization for a redefinition of values, only to find an ages-old culture in flux and disruption for having indiscriminately embraced the very code he has rejected. Nothing short of a new definition of man would do.

In 1927, Malraux had also published a short essay "On European Youth" which sheds great light on the state of mind of his generation. And in just a handful of pages we find, at a stage of germination, certain major themes he had already isolated for a lifetime of exploration.

Proceeding again from the Nietzschean premise of the "death of God," Malraux recognizes man himself as the only valid "object" now worthy of our passion and our reflection. For centuries, christianity had provided not only the framework of western civilization but the frame of reference for our values, our world-view, and our perception of self, including in particular our criteria of artistic creation and our standards of moral conduct. In Malraux's view, the christian framework may still prevail—as a form, christianity has not altogether crumbled—but its spell no longer binds us. Once subject, we are now free, free not to believe and to accept the consequences of our disbelief, our isolation from the gods. It is easy to detect here the basic argument on which the existentialism of the 1950s will be predicated.

Malraux writes fervently of our "deliverance"—not only from christianity but from the whole apparatus of western civilization—and urges his contemporaries to "take full cognizance" of their status and forge a working new concept of man, a new vision of reality, and a freshly wrought set of civilization values. What will be this new "notion?" he asks rhetorically, that will restore the "unity" once provided by our christian faith? Although he sees the myth of God as having left a profoundly engraved "wound" on man, Malraux does not entirely despair: "We intuit our existence only by the wounds we bear." Nor does he write of the church with the anti-clerical fanaticism of an eighteenth century *philosophe* or a latter-day atheist. He neither raves, rants, nor vilifies; with cool lucidity, he appraises what appears to be man's present fate, and accepts our "deliverance" as a philosophic point of departure for an urgently needed new system of thought.

With olympian distance, he reviews the key stages of man's view of man from the unifying faith of the Middle Ages to the present "disorder." It is "individualism" (as we have seen in Malraux's novels) that is the villain. The nineteenth century, inheriting romantic new notions of "sensibility," gave unprecedented stature to the concept of each *individual* self, resulting in a chaotic dispersion of "selves" wherein no universal concept of man and no structured relationship between abstract principle and concrete action any longer exists. This, coupled with the simultaneous demise of Christendom, leaves man "garbed in the rags of his former gods," and in need of clothing himself anew, now that our heroic dreams have turned to dust.

Malraux writes, and purports to speak for all of us, like one who has passed through a crucial illness and is now entering a convalescence from which a wholly new being will emerge. He proposes no easy formula, only guidelines. Self-worship having expended itself, we must turn away from narcissistic introspection and "detach ourselves from self," exploring in *action* new "possibilities" of man, heretofore unknown or unrealized. What is strongly suggested is that this new order of man will be a *collective* one and thereby lead to a restructured notion of fundamental man.

It is in this essay on European youth that Malraux first set forth the idea of human "fraternity" as the way out of despair. And from these basic ideas, bold metaphysical stuff on the part of a literary tyro, would come the six novels of André Malraux wherein individual man is pitted against his collective counterpart. We find here too the philosophic and esthetic underpinnings on which

Malraux would later construct his massive Olympian commentary on art and civilization.

Writing at mid-point between the late nineteenth century works of Dostoyevsky and Nietzsche and the advent of the existentialist movement, Malraux showed extraordinary perception in pinpointing the philosophic agony that leads from *The Brothers Karamazov* and *Thus Spake Zarathustra* to the writings of Sartre and Camus. Man's isolation from old gods and the need for a viable new faith has seldom been so incisively stated as in this essay. Written at mid-point between two world wars as well, it sums up with admirable succinctness the moral dilemma of thinking European youth at a crucial moment in intellectual history.

Urging his generation to go forth and do battle in 1927, Malraux was ostensibly characterizing a *spirit* of "revolt" and encouraging participation in a "revolution" only vaguely delineated. Looking back to that time from our present vantage point, one has the impression that he was almost intuitively forecasting his own particular destiny. He had observed at close hand a more specific revolutionary restlessness in the east: the *Jeune Annam* of Indochina, one of the first "national liberation" movements destined to leave a scar on history in the 1960s, and the uprising in China that would culminate in the communizing of that nation in 1949. No one could yet fully forecast the direction these early manifestations would take. Nor could André Malraux, in 1927, have any inkling that in less than ten years he would find himself —like American novelist Ernest Hemingway and British writers George Orwell, W.H. Auden, Stephen Spender, and Christopher Isherwood—on the battlefields of Spain, nor that soon after the world would explode into the mightiest war in history, between freedom and fascism.

Yet with remarkable intuition he already sensed that vast transformation was imminent and that revolution rather than evolution would be the tenor of our century. It was simply too soon to predict the exact shape of events in which the youth he sought to rally would come to "do battle." And much too soon to imagine that he, André Malraux, would become a legend in his era, encounter another legendary figure, and join forces in an epic political battle.

9

An Encounter of Legends

When General Charles De Gaulle, provisional president of post-war France, met with André Malraux in August 1945, it was the encounter of two legends. The De Gaulle legend began on June 18, 1940, when, in opposition to the Nazi puppet government of Vichy, De Gaulle made a radio broadcast from London naming himself leader in exile of "Free French" forces. It was a boldly dramatic gesture (not unlike General MacArthur's "I shall return"), all the more so since De Gaulle was only a brigadier general and undersecretary of war when France surrendered to Germany, with no official authority to take such a step. But it was the kind of heroically theatrical gesture designed to inspire a world in chaos, and a gesture that would assuredly excite the forty year old Malraux, once self-appointed commander of an air squadron in Spain but in 1940 a common French soldier in a Nazi prison camp.

The "man of June 18th," as the French press would come to identify De Gaulle after the war, was seeking out cabinet members and staff to form his new government; through mutual associates, the meeting with Malraux had been arranged. It is believed that Malraux, after his prison escape, had had some thought of fleeing to London in September 1940. There is also a tale that he had later attempted to communicate with the General, offering his services to the Free French air force, but this mid-August meeting of 1945 was their first. More than an encounter of legends, it was an encounter of destinies, for the two men, seemingly worlds apart in background and philosophy, were to become closely allied for the next twenty five years in one of the most extravagant political adventures of our time.

There is no doubt that General De Gaulle was impressed by Malraux's personal dynamism, the qualities of his mind, his reputation as a writer, and his role in the underground resistance. But what of his radical political ties, his reputation as an alleged communist or fellow traveler? Convinced that Malraux posed no "threat" to the Gaullist moderate-to-right political program, that his loyalty could be counted on, De Gaulle and his advisors, in an astutely Machiavellian move, adopted André Malraux as a symbol. His presence at De Gaulle's side was meant to allay fears that a right-wing general was seizing power, and Malraux was further assigned to actively court the political left without which the General could not expect to rally the French electorate.

In their first brief interview, De Gaulle must also have sensed Malraux's qualities as an orator, and over the years to come, Malrucian rhetoric was to be heard over and over again, throughout France and throughout the world, preaching the virtues and the historical necessity of Gaullism. The first chapter of this political alliance was astonishingly short. In the October 1945 election, despite a heavy pro-communist vote, there emerged a socialist-moderate coalition favorable to General De Gaulle, and on November 13, he became head of state. Then, in a surprise move, on January 26, 1946, he resigned.

The history of Gaullist politics is almost unbearably complex. It centers essentially on two characteristics: a philosophy rooted in hypocritical myth, a politics of expediency rooted in "spoiled child" psychology.

1. *The Myth.* Based on his legendary heroism and his towering aura of authority, General De Gaulle was depicted as the natural savior of post-war France. His

immediate philosophical stance, the recurring theme of Gaullist propaganda, was to blame the country's woes on political factionalism: there were too many parties quarreling among themselves, ambitious for power rather than eager to serve the nation; only a "strong man" backed by the support of the people could rule, returning France to her former glory and destiny. This of course smacked of dictatorship, and further acted to splinter dissension. A corollary to this argument, as incredibly naive as it may seem, was that Gaullism was not a political movement, not a "party" in the usual sense, but a movement to embody the spirit of the French nation. This despite the fact that Frenchmen were asked to vote for Gaullist candidates in elections where they opposed existing political parties.

2. *The Psychology.* Capitalizing on post-war fears of a communist take-over in France or throughout Europe, and on the widespread fear of a World War III, the Gaullists devised a daredevil strategy: since only the "man of June 18th" could lead France, the opposition must cease and desist their quibbling, and heed the people's will. In brief, if the game were not played by the General's rules, the General would not play at all. Hence his resignation and retirement in January 1946, after only two months in command.

As Gaullist propagandist in the fall of 1945 and over the years to come, André Malraux served in very large measure to help manufacture the Gaullist myth, and to forge the strategy that brought De Gaulle back to power in 1958 for an extraordinary ten-year reign. His motives in so doing perplexed many historians and critics at the time; in retrospect it seems clear that Gaullism provided Malraux a fresh opportunity to be true to one of the driving forces of his psychological make-up: translating a philosophic faith into terms of action, just as he and his fictional heroes had done on other battlefields.

De Gaulle ostensibly "retired" to write his memoirs. Malraux, as we have seen, set about working on the series of art books meant to crown his career as a "civilizationalist." But General De Gaulle's dire prediction proved accurate: France swiftly fell into a whirlwind of political turmoil that would result, during the next twelve years, in a rapid succession of rise-and-fall governments, and long stretches of time with no government at all.

In April 1947, the General made his move. In the shadow of the cathedral at Strasbourg, where he had two years earlier participated in a victory mass, De Gaulle made a resounding speech proclaiming the formation of the R.P.F.—*Rassemblement du Peuple Français*, which was to serve, if not as a Gaullist party, as a "rallying" or "reunion" of the French people, their vehicle for expressing the national will that a Gaullist regime assure the destiny of France.

For Frenchmen, Strasbourg has a very particular semiotic value. It is the principal city of Alsace-Lorraine, the territory so hotly contended by France and Germany since the Franco-Prussian War of 1870, and thereby a symbol of fierce nationalism. De Gaulle himself—like France's earlier savior, Joan of Arc—was a native of Lorraine. Dunkirk-born Malraux, in a telling example of his fact-or-fiction fancy, had "adopted" Alsace-Lorraine as his homeland by creating the Berger family of his last novel, *Les Noyers de l'Altenburg*, in which the Strasbourg cathedral embodies fundamental and everlasting Man. Then, in the closing days of the war, as the Resistance "Colonel Berger," he had created an Alsace-Lorraine Brigade responsible for "mopping up" operations in that section of France, driving the last Germans from French soil. In 1948, the agnostic Malraux chose Strasbourg cathedral as the setting of his second marriage; in a gesture of medieval tradition, he wedded his half-brother Roland's widow, Madeleine, and adopted her two sons. In the early days of Gaullism, both De Gaulle and Malraux took pains to be portrayed as bearing the "cross of Lorraine" while fiddling French politicians fiddled.

"Malraux the Fascinator"—such was the accusatory title of one article in the magazine *Esprit* which devoted its entire October 1948 issue to André Malraux whose allegiance to De Gaulle had become, among intellectuals, as great a question for controversy as the question of De Gaulle himself was for all France. The articles represented a wide spectrum of opinion. Admirers of Malraux, as might be expected, conjured up his greatness as a writer and his heroic humanism as a champion of just causes. Some defended his presence at the heart of the Gaullist movement; others seemed to rest their case on the argument that his credentials as a liberal were unquestioned despite the seeming implications of his new alliance. To intellectuals of a right-wing bent, he was seen either as a repentent sinner or a man whose left-wing politics were still suspect. Arch-leftists and some moderates, however, deplored the treason that seemed implicit in his Gaullist affiliation. Their articles on "le cas Malraux" ranged from deep disappointment over his "change" of political stripe to outraged attacks of heresy. Not only De Gaulle but Malraux himself was charged with fascism. The most biting attack was that of Claude-Edmonde Magny, the author of "Malraux the Fascinator," who unhesitatingly found in Malraux traces of fraudulent intellectualism and outright opportunism.

It was at this point in the history of ideas that Jean-Paul Sartre had advanced, as one of the tenets of Existentialism, the concept of "bad faith," and it was shocking to contemplate what Magny strongly suggested, that Malraux, the twentieth century's outspoken champion of man, might be guilty not only of a breach of credo but inherent "bad faith." Undaunted, if not unwounded, by such attacks, Malraux held unswervingly to his Gaullist faith and became its foremost crusader.

During De Gaulle's first brief rule, Malraux had held the title "Minister of Information," but the function of propagandist. Fiction became "fact;" the novelist found himself playing the role of his anonymous narrator in *Les Conquérants* who served Garine in that capacity. Malraux held a higher view of his ministry, however, and entertained grandiose notions of extending "information" into the cultural and educational domains; but all this had been aborted by the General's abrupt resignation.

When De Gaulle subsequently announced the formation of the R.P.F., propagandist Malraux christened that launching as "the crossing of the Rubicon." Anti-Gaullists, convinced of General De Gaulle's totalitarianism, would not take kindly to the reference to Caesar—but this was a bold and often reckless game. Some years later, in a shift of metaphor, Malraux characterized the Gaullists' long struggle for power as "the crossing of the desert"—but the apparent reference to Moses's miracle seemed to suggest a more contemporary miracle. Malraux's anti-Stalinism did not extend to Chinese communism, and one could not help thinking of Mao's "Long March" as the crossing that led to the victory of communism in Peking. It was just such a Gaullist victory in France that gripped Malraux's imagination.

To this effort, he brought not only ardor but skill, imagination, and new American-style promotional techniques. Malraux introduced public opinion polls and profited from his experience as an art editor to produce bold, colorful, patriotic posters. He edited first a newssheet, then a Gaullist propaganda magazine, and also devised a fund-raising public relations scheme whereby the people were asked to send a fifty franc stamp to the General at his country estate, symbolizing their collective will for his leadership.

Malraux's greatest fervor was reserved for the platform. He staged a continuous round of rallies, sometimes with De Gaulle as speaker, more often with himself as spokesman. Seldom using a text or even notes, he relied on his prodigious memory and natural verbosity to produce a relentless flow of rhetoric contrived to "captivate" rather than "persuade" his audience. Too frequently his oratory betrayed its sham incoherence, revealing in this demigod of French thought and letters a dangerous streak of demagoguery—not destined to enchant the Parisian intellectual Left. Nevertheless, municipal, regional, even national elections continued to favor substantial percentages of R.P.F. candidates in 1947 and 1948, but the personal mandate General De Gaulle awaited was not forthcoming. By 1950 the party was clearly on the wane, and by 1953 in virtual eclipse.

Yet five years later, when the French-Algerian crisis exploded, the Gaullist silence was not only broken, De Gaulle found himself almost unexpectedly in power again. While extreme radical groups in Algeria called for "national liberation," millions of *colons* (Algerians of French rather than Arab descent) stood fast for dominion by France. The situation, somewhat analogous to that of Europeans in South African countries or Americans in the Canal Zone, actually triggered events that more closely resembled those of the Spanish Civil War. The French Army Generals in Algeria, following General Franco's move in Spain, threatened not only insurrection but the invasion of mainland France. De Gaulle was deemed the only leader capable of staving off chaos and took office, with sweeping powers in June, 1958. With him for the next decade, as Minister of Cultural Affairs, was André Malraux, whose activities during that period seem sadly tame compared to his earlier crusades.

As a modest microcosm of his "Imaginary Museum" concept, Malraux was able to exert some influence on educational reform: the introduction of audio-visual methods for teaching art, history, and such. A more ambitious extension of the idea was his determined foundation of a series of "Maisons de la Culture" throughout France . . . centers where reproductions of artistic masterpieces could be viewed by all the people (who would presumably come to appreciate them as they had come to appreciate De

Gaulle). Malraux also "loaned" the Venus de Milo and the Mona Lisa, two non-French masterpieces of the French national treasury, to museums in other lands. Ironically, just as Mussolini is often remembered as having made Italian trains run on time, Minister Malraux is remembered by some Frenchmen as having inaugurated the cleaning up of Paris monuments and buildings, gray with the patina of time.

More rewarding, one might assume, were his duties as a roving Gaullist ambassador. The intimate conversations with world leaders Nehru, Mao, and many others (including General De Gaulle himself), his consultations with Kennedy and Nixon, a pro-Gaullist rally in Guadaloupe—these are the stuff of which Malraux's political memoirs are made. From adolescence, perhaps earlier, André Malraux had aspired to high adventure and high places.

Did Malraux harbor still higher political ambition? Did he perhaps see himself as De Gaulle's successor? There is no evidence of the latter, though some of his enemies feared it. As to his diplomatic aspirations, it was at least rumored that he really sought a ministerial post involving Algeria or Indochina. But it is also generally accepted that Malraux periodically refused De Gaulle's encouragement to run for office as an R.P.F. candidate. This, given Malraux's temperament, his pride, his sense of legend, seems consistent. Why seek modest public office at the risk of losing? Why indeed seek any higher responsibility? As a trusted confidant of a world leader, soldier and statesman whom he revered and believed in as a man of destiny, Malraux apparently found the role that gratified his sense of grandeur for twenty-three years, from 1945 to 1968. As American journalist Murray Kempton shrewdly observed of De Gaulle and Malraux, "They are so much more wonderful than anyone real."

While it is easy to understand Malraux's fascination with Gaullism as an exercise in power control, the translation of a philosophy into action, it is not easy to fathom his unexpected devotion to this particular figure, Charles De Gaulle. Yet on reviewing Malraux's evolution as a thinker and writer, we find, in spite of apparent shifts and surprises, the consistent quest for an absolute that De Gaulle somehow embodied. Malraux's search for a meaningful new concept of man, developed in *Les Noyers de l'Altenburg*, is already apparent in his 1927 essay addressed to European youth. This need for a metaphysical renovation is also evident in the still earlier *Tentation de l'Occident*. Essentially, the only "drastic change" in Malraux's writings over half a century is the gradual shift of interest and emphasis from a prototype individualist (the "conqueror") to men collectively, and finally to Man representing humankind. Within that tripartite pattern, though, there is an inherent duality that provides the tension of Malraux's thought: the tension between the individual and his collective counterpart. (Garine does not "represent" the people with whom he fights, as Kyo does instinctively and as Manuel learns to in his hard-won efforts to earn leadership.) From that Hegelian opposition there subsequently emerges a synthesis: the individual who does incarnate a collective will.

With this "leader" paradigm in mind, present in Malraux's thinking from the start, one more readily acknowledges his mythical De Gaulle. One may further conjecture that he "chose" De Gaulle not so much for his controversial qualities or policies, but because he was *there*: the one man, as Gaullist propaganda kept repeating, who was capable of inspiring—or imposing—French unity. Malraux, never a communist or thoughtfully dedicated marxist, had worked side by side with communists, marxists, and anarchists in the Orient, in Spain, and in France, not because he shared their political proposals or strategies but because he shared their avowed ideals of justice and humanity, and perhaps even more because they were *there*, virtually the only ones at the time fighting injustice and oppression, and seeking a new appraisal of the body social, a new vision of man. It is difficult withal, indeed arduous, for most of us to find in the haughty, often tedious, frequently pompous, public De Gaulle with his antique style and rhetoric, the leader of today or tomorrow that Malraux professed to discover.

When General De Gaulle again resigned in June, 1969, virtually driven from office by the recurring chaos of factionalism, the mounting discontent of the electorate, and finally the student riots of the previous year, Malraux once again followed. Time and again he had proclaimed "No Gaullism without De Gaulle," although that is just what French politics attempted. Reading Malraux's transcripts of private conversations with the General in December of 1969, one is awed by the depth of Malraux's belief in the man, which, in our own disbelief, appears not so much a faith but merely *blind* faith. To account for this, we must look back to a significant change in Malraux's personal evolution, his metamorphosis from internationalist to nationalist.

In his twenties, he was but one of a whole generation rejecting European values centered chiefly on individualism, and in search of exoticism and "otherness," perhaps a new kind of "oneness." In the east, and again in Spain, he came to know a new kind of mystique, the fraternity of human will, yet brotherhood notwithstanding, the people were not his own; he was a stranger. While men may sometimes discover their identity and "homeland" far from home, it seems that final self-revelation came to Malraux with the fall of France in 1940. One has only to reread the "cathedral scenes" in *Les Noyers de l'Altenburg*, his last novel and the only one on France. Chartres to the West, Strasbourg to the East, this is Malraux's newfound universe, where those monuments of medieval France tower mightily and speak symbolically of a people, his own, unheeded by the younger Malraux. It took a great world holocaust for him to recognize in their centuries-old Gothic statues the faces of his contemporary countrymen.

If Malraux the novelist were to create a fictional leader for modern-day France, would he not have conjured up a figure of cathedral-like proportions, speaking in cadences of antique French, one who shared the province of Saint Joan, whose Christian name he shared with Carlus Magnus, Charlemagne, and whose patronymic proclaimed his advent as Charles of Gaul?

Malraux seems in almost mystical fashion to have believed that General Charles De Gaulle did embody the spirit of France, and saw in him an authentic man of destiny, a latter-day Conqueror. But as Malraux had foreseen forty years before, and forecast in his early works, our traditional western concept of man, gods, and demigods was undergoing an identity crisis. The twentieth century was not to be an age of the grandiose.

10

The "Fascinator"

The most talked-about literary event in 1967 in France was the publication of Malraux's *Antimémoires* (Anti-Memoirs). It had been known for some time that the elder statesman and patriarch of French letters was writing a book about his life, and the *Antimémoires* became an instant best-seller. Amidst praise in some quarters for the imaginative style and power of Malraux's writing, there was also a good deal of disappointment and confusion. This was also true in English-speaking countries when the book appeared in translation the following year.

Many readers and critics, who perhaps should have known better, somehow assumed that Malraux would "tell all," that the facts behind the legend would now be revealed and the record set straight. Such was far from the case. "Man is more than just a little pile of secrets," Malraux had written in *Les Noyers de l'Altenburg*, and he had no intention here of indulging in the intimacies and personal revelations that are the stock and trade of conventional autobiography. As the perversely curious title indicated, these were to be something ohter than "memoirs."

In the first few pages, Malraux explains his case. "I do not like my youth," he bluntly states. The book therefore goes no further back in time than Malraux's first trip to the east—and very little is said about that by way of direct reference. Why "*anti*-memoirs?" Because this book "answers a question that Memoirs do not ask without answering the questions usually raised." It is one of Malraux's most elusive and elliptical utterances. Two other statements, however, make perfectly clear his intentions and his choice of title:

"The play of memory does not necessarily reconstruct a life in chronological order."

"Certain of our dreams are just as meaningful as our recollections. And so I reproduce in these pages some scenes I once transformed into fiction."

The first alerts us that we are not going to read a sequential narrative; the second, that it is not going to be altogether factual.

A glimpse at the table of contents is as baffling at first as was the title of the book itself:

Les Noyers de l'Altenburg
Antimémoires
La Tentation de l'Occident
La Voie royale
La Condition humaine

One promptly notes that four of the five sections bear titles of previous works by Malraux, though not in the chronology of their publication. Just as Malraux the novelist had drawn from his experiences in the east and in Spain, now Malraux the memoirist uses his early fiction as both a source and a frame of reference for structuring this unorthodox set of recollections. It is this suggested interchange of fact and fancy that poses a teasing challenge for the reader of the *Antimémoires*.

The second most striking feature in the composition of the *Antimémoires* is its unorthodox temporal organization. In his early "documentary" novels, Malraux had employed the journalistic device of "datelines" not only to lend realism and authenticity, but to create on-going movement, time ticking away. Throughout the *Antimémoires*, his use of multiple-year headings (1923/1945 . . . 1934/1950/1965 . . . 1958/65) is calculated to evoke just the opposite effect: ever-shifting movement and perspective, back and forth in time. Malraux's purpose, not unlike that of Proust in *A la Recherche du temps perdu* (Remembrance of Things Past), is to reproduce a series of experiences from various points in time, endowing them with a simultaneity which the calendar defies but to which associative human memory permits access.

1965, somewhere off Crete gives us the "present" of the narrative, the moment in which the text is being written. Malraux had been ill and was now off on a long recuperative sea voyage to distant parts. En route, he allegedly received word from General De Gaulle asking him to undertake a kind of "mission" to India and China. Already, the alchemy is at work. We recall that in the opening scenes of *La Voie royale* and *Les Conquérants*, a westerner was heading east on shipboard. The ship on which Malraux is presently sailing, by extraordinary coincidence, is called the *Cambodia*.

A chapter heading such as *1948/1965* asks us to follow the vagaries of Malraux's thinking as he conjures up recollections of two different meetings he had with Indian premier Nehru. As one reads on, what is still more maddening—yet altogether fascinating—is that the section called *La Voie royale* deals only obliquely with Malraux's novel of that name, and that *La Condition humaine* focuses on Malraux's conversations in 1965 with Chou En-lai and Mao Tse-tung. True to his promise, Malraux fuses personal recollection with the creative *rêverie* that is fiction, and in so doing plays Proustian havoc with time and so-called "reality."

Les Noyers de l'Altenburg. The first part of this three-part opening section is a succinct recapitulation of key scenes from Malraux's earlier novel of the same name.

It deals briefly with the Grandfather's suicide, raising the fundamental question of individual destiny in an absurd universe: "The greatest mystery is not that we have been flung at random between the profusion of matter and the stars, but that within this prison we can draw from ourselves images powerful enough to deny our nothingness." The theme of creating "images" that defy "nothingness" and thereby define man, their creator, had come increasingly to haunt Malraux and dominate his later work.

The scene of the colloquium in the Altenburg library, greatly reduced here, loses much of its ironic impact, but the final tableau of Vincent Berger wandering forth among the walnut trees at sundown is transcribed almost verbatim from the novel and shows to what degree Malraux was also haunted by man face to face with brute nature: that forest of trees from which we fabricate libraries, firewood, and the statues of saints. It is difficult for the reader not to reflect that from trees also comes the paper on which men construct monuments in words.

Malraux then abruptly abandons the pseudo-autobiographical narrative that constituted the novel of this name; he ceases to be the Alsatian Berger and becomes the "real" Malraux, reflecting on the panorama of civilizations. His extraordinarily associative mind leaps irrepressibily through time and space. The pyramids of Egypt become the pyramids of Mexico, and these in turn are metamorphosed into modern-day museums. Versailles is also such a museum, history transformed into a monument. And in Malraux's volatile psyche, the glory of Versailles suggests the ignominy of St. Helena, and Napoleon emerges as Hitler. It is a tour de force of verbal "trick photography."

Not surprisingly, these seemingly random musings are governed by a single prototype altogether familiar to readers of Malraux: the legendary conquering hero. Against the horizon of imposing pyramids and the grandiose architecture of Versailles, we perceive a parade of ghosts, like so many dusty sun gods: the pharaohs, kings, and emperors who had shaped the course of history from 1965 B.C. to 1965 A.D. ("Time's symmetry has often haunted me"), and find their common commemoration within the walls of museums: "I like eccentric museums because they seem to be playing a game with eternity."

To round out his conqueror/monument pattern, Malraux returns to one of his own legendary exploits, the 1934 flight over Arabia in search of the temple of Sheba. Since we know that Malraux had "borrowed" from that experience to create the flight scene in *Le Temps du mépris*, it is not surprising that his present account now reads like fiction, seeming to "borrow" from the novel. Demonstrating the element of reality and irreality present in both fact and fiction, Malraux states that the "reality" he wanted to express in both cases was the sensation of "returning to earth." It is essentially a psychological reality, he seems to imply, outside the limits of time, as words are.

Antimémoires. Within the framework of this book called *Antimémoires*, the longest single section is that called "Antimémoires." While this unit is something of a mirror of the whole, it would be presumptuous, given Malraux's sleight-of-pen technique, to assume that it is necessarily the "key" segment. If one is looking for revelations beyond those already apparent in Malraux's novels, one must look deeper than the surface of any one section to the cyclical recurrence of themes and patterns, verbal structures and visual tableaux. In this section, the conqueror image is once more identifiable with the presence of De Gaulle and Nehru, in passing references to Churchill, Lawrence of Arabia, Lenin, Trotsky, and Stalin, and, significantly, in Malraux's version of his own imminent death before a firing squad.

In these pages, Malraux dances across history from 1923, when he first visited India, to 1958, when he returned there as De Gaulle's official emissary. His impressionistic recollection of that 1923 visit is rooted in a recognizable Malrucian tableau: "an imperial avenue had existed here in the days of the Moguls, and trees no longer grew in the soil which had once been tramped down." It is the world of "the royal way," Malraux's ideogram for grandeur and decadence, and for man's struggle to retain the primacy of civilization against the encroachment of the jungle. This presupposes the daring, the cunning and the leadership of a popular hero, and Malraux's tripartite hero is composed here of General De Gaulle, Prime Minister Nehru, and Malraux himself.

De Gaulle is seen as the sole liberator who can unify post-war France and move her people forward to greatness, dependent neither on the east nor the west. Malraux's summary of his initial encounters with the General is a mixture of modesty and immodesty:

"General De Gaulle asks in the name of France if you will help him."

"I have a tendency to think myself useful."

Nehru is seen as wearing the mantle of Mahatma Gandhi, a latter-day saint who piously incarnates not only the will but also the soul of a people. But when Malraux writes of Nehru, "He was creating India while surrounded by a Saturn's Ring of hostile politicians . . ." we have only to substitute "France" for "India' to discern that the Gandhi/Nehru figure is actually Charles De Gaulle. One may also make the same substitution in this statement:

"He pitied India. He knew its misery. But he wanted to see it committed to a unique destiny, dedicated to becoming the conscience of the world."

It is not that Malraux is insensitive to Nehru's uniqueness as a leader and an individual, nor does he fail to appreciate the singularity of India's social, economic, and political problems. He writes of these with keen insight. Beyond this portrait, nonetheless, lies Malraux's abiding image of the Ideal Liberator, and his quixotic quest for the leader who embodies an entire people. Having evoked the concept of "liberation," Malraux passes easily to the liberation of France at the end of world war II. The imprisonment of both Gandhi and Nehru by British authorities somehow conjures Malraux's own prison camp experiences of 1940 and 1944—and to some extent perhaps De Gaulle's exile during the war years.

In the lightest of terms, but not without a certain comic opera bravoura, Malraux describes several brushes with death before what he describes as a "burlesque firing squad" and a "mock execution." However true Malraux's telling may be, this is assuredly another version of Perken facing the armed tribesmen in *La Voie royale*, the Chinese and Spanish revolutionaries being gunned down in *La Condition humaine* and *L'Espoir*. But this "true life" autobiographical rendering of one man's fate also closely parallels *Le Temps du mépris* in which the hero succeeds in *escaping* death—liberated to join a resistance in the cause of liberating others.

Compounding the interplay of reality and romance, the narrating Malraux has once again become "Berger," assuming the name of one of his own fictional characters. Colonel Berger, however, is not unlike Malraux's idealization of De Gaulle; he is chosen leader by popular acclaim: "Berger in Command! Berger! Berger!" Malraux has stressed the extraordinary length to which the early events of one's life may foreshadow and prefigure later events. Perhaps objectively true in some instances, it is not altogether astonishing when the creator of fiction composes a perverse form of autobiography wherein the chapters take their titles from his novels.

La Tentation de l'Occident. At the center of his *Antimémoires,* Malraux has situated a meditation on death.

The title of this section derives from the first major work he had published, contrasting the values and ideals of Oriental and Occidental civilization, yet underscoring a certain magnetism drawing each to the other despite their powerful polarization. It is now India rather than China that holds his gaze; in particular, the tenets of Hindu, Buddhist, and Brahman religious thought which he finds paradoxically appealing:

> "O my god who art only myself"
>
> "Deathless, birthless, unchanging forever"
>
> "Who can kill immortality?"
>
> "Certain is death for all who shall be born,
> And certain is birth for all who have died . . ."

Malraux is no longer so much "tempted" by the perplexities of an alien philosophical mode; rather, he finds here the echo of a notion he had stumbled upon early in life and developed elaborately in his writings on art: that other civilizations serve most dramatically to shed light on one's own. He also rediscovers at the root of Hindu thinking an idea he had long cherished in his novels, that death gives new meaning to life. And he uses this as a transition to reconstruct the final scene from the last of those novels, *Les Noyers de l'Altenburg*, in which Berger and his comrades, in 1945, escape from being trapped in their tank and emerge to view the world in fresh terms: "Thus it was, perhaps, that God looked at the first man."

La Voie royale. In this "fourth act" of his narrative, Malraux takes time out for comedy. It is here that his free-wheeling interplay of fact and fiction takes on its most flagrant, indeed outrageous, guise. His ship, the *Cambodia* (hence the mythic incarnation of his first ill-fated trip eastward in the 1920s), has symbolically collided with an oil tanker in the Singapore harbor. It is July 14, and the festivities of the French colony render this once-Chinese city even more cosmopolitan than it had become over the decades. Although the tone of the narrative is allegedly *verismo*, Malraux sees emerging from the crowd to greet him the Baron de Clappique—who is, of course, the memorable tragi-comic figure of *La Condition humaine*.

The reader is thus faced, in a work of ostensibly autobiographical intent, with the supposedly "real" encounter of an author with one of his fictional characters. This occurs in a section called *La Voie royale*, although that is not even the novel in which Clappique had appeared. Clappique, it seems, wishes to discuss with the narrator, his creator, the prospect of making a film (just as Malraux had filmed one of his own novels in Spain). The film is to be called "The Royal Way," dealing with the exploits of the legendary European adventurer Mayrena. Mayrena, we recall, was a shadowy presence in Malraux's novel, *La Voie royale*, and that novel, just to complete this game of mirrors, was the fictionalized version of Malraux's own exploits in the jungles of Cambodia!

Clappique's alleged scenario is a merciless traversty of a novel Malraux seems never to have cared much for, one that he virtually disavowed. These pages are more than a gratuitously burlesque exorcism, however. By confronting himself with a possible alter ego, Clappique, and having the ghost of Mayrena hover over them both, Malraux seems to reveal himself in a rare moment of candor and self-examination. A far cry from either the daredevil of the flight over Sheba, or the illustrious emissary to Nehru's India, Malraux glimpses himself briefly as the charlatan con-artist Clappique, an undaunted fool of fate, and simultaneously as the archetypal "conqueror" Mayrena, also fate's fool.

La Condition humaine. Malraux's final destination on this 1965 journey, which also proved an odyssey of memory, was China. His conversation with Chairman Mao, however undramatic in terms of foreign policy, is undoubtedly of historical and political interest, and it does reflect Malraux's abiding obsession with "the temptation of the west." This final section of the *Antimémoires* is more intriguing, however, as part of the over-all design of the work: an experiment in the simultaneity of fact and fiction, and the freely associated superimposition of the structures of memory.

When Malraux's ship stops at Hong Kong, he inevitably recalls his oft-recounted visit there to acquire typographer's lettering needed for his news-publishing venture in Vietnam. (Or was that alleged visit a creation of the imagination that he had himself come to believe?) However elusive the legend, it is altogether certain that Malraux, the propagandist for Annamite self-determination, was destined to become propagandist for De Gaulle and the R.P.F. following the liberation of France. Thus we find inseparably joined in Malraux's *Antimémoires* the foolhardy young antiestablishment "conqueror" of the Temple at Banteai-Srey and the accredited Gaullist emissary to the east in 1958: ". . . all my surviving memories commune with one another. . . ."

Returning to France "over the Pole," the icy whiteness conjures up a December night when Malraux had delivered an oration commemorating the transfer to the Pantheon of the ashes of a fellow Resistance fighter. This memory, in turn, cinematically "dissolves" to another wartime recollection as the cavernous Pantheon suddenly seems to become the pre-historic caves of Lascaux, where ancestors of today's French people first created images of life on cold, hard, yet infinitely durable stone. Malraux's "antimemory" can carry him no further than this everrecurring symbol of everconstant, everchanging man. It was in just such caves that the *maquis*, the French underground fighters, hid from the enemy in their struggle for liberation.

Despite its consciously discursive complexities and the fact that it overtly "reveals" nothing of Malraux the man, the *Antimémoires* does reveal a tightly knit schema of personal obsessions that serve to identify Malraux's temperament as thinker and writer. None of its facets is really new to Malraux's readers, but their codified presence in a single "first person" work at least serves to reinforce the structure of his psyche, and, in turn, recreates the schema of his career. Here then are several of the dominant thought-structures recurring throughout Malraux's fiction and nonfiction, and which are found in various combinatory clusters throughout the pages of Malraux's *Antimémoires.*

1. *The "conquering hero."* From his first novel on, Malraux had explored the psychological and metaphysical nature of conquest, finding in traditional concepts of "heroism" a void—attractive for its flamboyant *farfelu* individualism, but nonetheless a void. Despite the seemingly definitive implications of *La Condition humaine*, a celebration of fraternal collectivity, Malraux nonetheless returns nostalgically to the solitary conqueror figure in his *Antimémoires.* Along with the legendary Mayrena, there are frequent glimpses of Napoleon and other iconoclastic *mythomanes.* Malraux is also naturally fascinated with the legend of Rimbaud, the dazzling poetic genius who gave up writing at age nineteen for a life of uncertain adventure in Africa. Even when he writes of Nehru or Mao, Malraux seems less to admire the world leader than the daredevil "soldier of fortune" in these men, who in their earlier years had been outcasts of the social order, recklessly facing prison and death in order to lead a movement of liberation.

2. *Escape from death.* Starting with the hero figures of Malraux's first two novels, men challenge death and die, denied that one truly meaningful conquest. But in *La Condition humaine* and *L'Espoir*, although men die in considerable numbers, Malraux implies a transcendent "conquest" over death in that each individual death endows the individual's life with meaning and dignity. It is only in *Le Temps du mépris* and *Les Noyers de l'Alten-*

burg that man literally escapes from death and undergoes a neo-Christian rebirth wherein life takes on a new aura. Returning to this theme in his *Antimémoires* and despite what he states to the contrary (". . . dying seemed banal to me. What interested me was Death"), Malraux seems to accept death as an abstraction, a phenomenon to ruminate, and yet believe in his own cat-like immortality. Devoting a dozen pages to his death-defying flight over Sheba, he revels in his daredevil escape. He virtually mocks death when faced with a firing squad, and invokes an inexplicit deus ex machina to save Berger and his comrades in the tank episode taken from *Les Noyers de l'Altenburg*. We find in this urgent life-wish an echo of the Hindu chant: "Who can kill immortality?"

3. *Conversations with greatness.* Akin to immortality lies eternal wisdom, and so throughout Malraux's work we are privy to weighty reflections on man, his gods, his demons, and his universe, set forth by a venerable sage figure. The wise old Chinese in *La Tentation de l'Occident*, father Gisors in *La Condition humaine*, and Alvear in *L'Espoir* are all variations on the theme of the scholar-teacher to whom young men listen as guides and mentors. In *Les Voix du Silence* and its companion volumes, Malraux modulates from dialogue to monologue and assumes the role of patriarch himself. His role in the *Antimémoires* is once again that of listener, or, more precisely, as intermediary between De Gaulle and the elder statesmen of the east whose guest he is.

Malraux never sought political office himself as some thought—and others feared—he might do. It is altogether clear, however, that he was fascinated by the acquiring and wielding of power. He was that rare "conquering hero" who was content to bathe in reflected glory and let the rays of the sun-gods glance becomingly off his visor.

4. *Caves, tombs, and museums.* It is by no mere accident of the associative process that Malraux's *Antimémoires* ends with an anecdote of the prehistoric Lascaux

caves. Their walls are the repository of prehistoric art, a testimony of man's earliest efforts to shape an image of his existence. No theme had consumed Malraux more earnestly since world war II than the philosophy—or as he chooses to call it, the "psychology"—of art: the creative act as a conquest over death, including the death of civilizations.

These final pages therefore lead us directly back to earlier sections of the *Antimémoires* where Malraux meditates on the passage of men and of empires, the ruins that are buried and those fragmentary remains we house in museums. Tombs too are revealing monuments to glories past, and so tombs find their justly recurring place in the *Antimémoires*, from the tombs of the pharaohs to the simpler graves of Gandhi and Nehru which Malraux does not fail to visit. "Monument" is a key metaphor throughout.

All autobiography is a form of monument, fashioned in the words and images of the writer's choosing. Although it is consciously unlike any traditional autobiography, *Antimémoires* is Malraux's projection of his life as *he* chose to remember it, part fact, part fiction, and as he chose to be remembered. In contrast to the custom of French poets who honor the memory of a writer by composing a *tombeau,* or tombstone, Malraux created his own *tombeau.* It is artistically crafted and carefully carries, in two-fold graphic unity, his own initials: *Antimémoires*, playing on the "A.M." in André Malraux.

11

Death and Metamorphosis

Just as *Les Voix du silence*, in 1951, had earned for novelist André Malraux a new kind of fame, so the *Anti-mémoires* of 1967 brought him renewed recognition, this time as a memoirist of stature. Throughout the last decade of his life, he continued vigorously to write and publish. Adventurer and editor, novelist and soldier, politician, essayist on civilization, government minister, Malraux had rarely been out of the limelight. During the years immediately following De Gaulle's retirement from politics, and his own, Malraux gave frequent interviews on the arts, world affairs, or his own life and work, to the press and on television. His opinions were constantly courted; except for a few dissenters, Malraux seemed to be *the* elder statesman and patriarch of letters.

But as the media are wont to do, they "overdid" Malraux; he became too much of a celebrity. Shortly after the election of Giscard d'Estaing, one periodical proclaimed, "It is too soon to judge Giscard, says André Malraux." One scarcely needed an intellect of Malraux's calibre to reach that conclusion, and such journalistic cheapness only served to diminish his stature. If television captured Malraux's experienced insights for millions of Frenchmen, it also cruelly captured the wrinkles, the paunchiness, and the almost frightening nervous tics that had grown aggravated with illness and age. Missing was the familiar cigarette; he had finally given them up. But it was rumored that he took drugs . . . had always been an opium addict. After all, went the logic of gossip, Malraux had lived in China as a youth. When war broke out in Bangladesh, his sudden bravura announcement that he was going to join India's fight had nothing of the ring of the Spanish Civil War years, and could only serve to make this septuagenarian look foolish in the eyes of many.

Yet if Malraux appeared in some ways diminished, his writings continued to burn with passion and intellect, more incisive, more paradoxical than ever. At the same time, quite understandably, his "old familiar friend," the spectre of death, loomed closer. In January 1970, Louise de Vilmorin, his constant companion for the past two years, suddenly died. They had met briefly in 1933, gone their separate ways, then met again and formed a devoted attachment. In November 1970, Malraux also lost the man to whom he had been most singularly devoted, General Charles De Gaulle. The giants of the century were beginning to pass: Nehru, Chou, Chiang, Franco, the painters Braque, Matisse, and Picasso; even to one who had stared death in the face, it must have seemed like the last act of history.

In 1971, Malraux published *Les Chênes qu'on abat* (Felled Oaks), his apologia for Gaullism and purportedly the record of his last conversation with the General—while snow falls heavily on the countryside, symbolic of the "snows of yesteryear." The death of Picasso prompted Malraux to write *La Tête d'obsidienne* (Picasso's Mask), a commemorative tribute to the great twentieth-century painter. In 1973, Malraux himself suffered near-paralysis and recorded his last escape from death in *Lazare* (Lazarus). Finally, in 1975, came *Hôtes de Passage* ("Transient Guests"), in which the legendary Alexander the Great emerges as yet another prototype of Malraux's obsession with conquerors, while the title suggests our ephemeral status as earthly creatures.

These four volumes were then incorporated into a

single volume intriguingly entitled *La Corde et les souris* (The Rope and the Mice).* The title is explained by a brief parable in which an artist is condemned to be hanged, his toes barely supporting his body. Fatigue will bring death. But true to his creative instinct, he sketches with one toe the figures of mice in the sand; the mice miraculously come to life and gnaw away the hangman's noose. Art as man's salvation has rarely been so powerfully conveyed.

On 23 November 1976, André Malraux died of pulmonary congestion in Paris, three weeks after reaching seventy-five, a birthday he had never really expected to see. In many world capitals, the report was gravely carried on the front page of leading newspapers like the *New York Times* which, in December 1923, had reported Malraux's first newsworthy exploit in the temples of Cambodia. The "bad boy" of Banteai Srey was now buried as an ex-minister of France. But posterity will likely little care about either of those titles; adventurers and statesmen are far easier to come by than poets who write parables about rope and mice.

Time magazine, in its memorial article, called Malraux "the last Renaissance figure." It is quite true that Malraux's interests and talents were myriad, his personality protean; despite his grim confrontation with twentieth-century realities, he also nurtured at heart a pan-European humanism with roots in the Renaissance. It is perhaps more revealing, withal, to see Malraux as the last of the romantic *poseurs*, in the lineage of Lord Byron, Chateaubriand, and Victor Hugo. Proud, defiant men, monumental literary figures with fighting political principles, each, like Malraux, let himself become cloaked in an aura of legend, legends to which their lives and

* Malraux designated *Antimémoires* as volume I and *La Corde et les souris* as volume II of his over-all last work with the inclusive title, *Le Miroir des Limbes* (The Mirror of Limbo).

works consciously contributed. In Malraux's case, reticence about his private life also left the door open to apocrypha.

Clara Malraux, in one of several books about life with her husband, describes one of their first outings together. On a dark night, in a low section of Paris, they are accosted by strange men; André pulls a gun from his pocket. Why he would have a gun is unexplained, seems indeed unaccountable. Is the episode true? Or is her memory merely dictating that this handsome young daredevil seemed the sort who *would* carry a weapon? Despite this speech by a character in *L'Espoir*, "I don't like guys who get their picture taken holding a gun," the legendary Malraux did seem to be pointing a revolver at the world. Elsewhere, unless Clara is romancing, it seems that André told her of translations he had allegedly done. While suitors may be permitted poetic license, one detects here a potential mythomania that would grow threateningly characteristic.

Malraux's most grievous breach with good faith was writing to American critic Edmund Wilson that he had served with the Kuomintang in Canton during the Chinese revolution. This of course does not diminish the artistry of *Les Conquérants* or *La Condition humaine* as works of the imagination; generally speaking, he maintained an oblique silence, neither denying nor affirming his alleged role. Extravagant as it may seem, one wonders if Malraux perhaps came to believe that he actually participated in the activities he described in his two China novels. And it was natural for readers who knew of Malraux's actual role in Spain to assume that he had also fought in China.

There are also aspects of Malraux's later political life that do little credit to him as a man. In the early days of the RPF, when Jean-Paul Sartre maintained a relentless attack on De Gaulle, Malraux apparently saw to it that Gallimard, both his publisher and Sartre's, would stop publishing Sartre's new review, *Les Temps Modernes*. In another example of political censorship, however, Malraux adopted the liberal cause. The government had banned a book called *La Question*, which exposed and protested the torture to which political prisoners in Algeria were being subjected. Malraux and Sartre both objected. Yet when De Gaulle was later ruling France, most liberals derided Minister Malraux for his silence on the torture question and his general endorsement of Algerian policy.

Malraux delighted in his ministerial functions: not only dictating national cultural platforms, but acting as confidant to the great and powerful. When he published his "conversations with De Gaulle," Malraux rather immodestly bemoaned the fact that Napoleon had had no great writer to record his thoughts on St. Helena. He must surely have been pleased, in 1972, when President Richard Nixon invited him to Washington for conferences prior to his now-famous China trip. A cartoon promptly appeared depicting a sober Nixon following Malraux's convoluted monologue on Chinese affairs, then mimicking it before a bemused Mao. If there is a role other than artist in which Malraux sought to portray himself, it was that of the "grey eminence."

Malraux's detractors, whether old political foes or brash young nihilists of the new student generation, liked to depict him as a "*fumiste*" or phoney, a hopeless *mythomane*. Mythmaker? Yes. *Mythomane*? No. Malraux does provide clues, however, that he is not unaware of a certain charlatanism in his temperamental make-up. His chosen epithet, "*farfelu*," suggests something of a carnival figure, a braggadocio daredevil whose word is subject to doubt. When the Baron de Clappique reappears in the *Antimémoires*—a fictional character chatting with his creator—he seems suspiciously like an alter ego. A third such presence in Malraux's work is that of the *shaman*: in slavic folklore, a conjuror or medicine man. In *Les Noyers de* *l'Altenburg*, Vincent Berger is identified as "a bit of a shaman," invoking the idea of the miracle worker who may, or may not, be a fakir.* Is Malraux intimating that, after all, Berger's truth may be only an illusion? Or, rather, by extension, that the artist himself is part soothsayer, part sorcerer?

Critic Claude-Edmonde Magny pejoratively accused Malraux of being a "fascinator"—which might also be a portrait of the artist. A dozen years before entering politics, the writer had written: "A political leader is necessarily an impostor." It is easier to understand the complexities of Malraux's temperament if one considers the various *shamans* who had first fascinated him.

Nietzsche and Dostoyevsky were two of the major influences that contributed to the formation of virtually every bright young French person of Malraux's generation, as indeed they had earlier influenced André Gide. In Dostoyevsky, young intellectuals found the irrational, the diabolical, and the mystical that were absent from their own neoclassical heritage. Malraux's enthusiasm for Dostoyevsky was unbounded, and is quite visible in the violent tensions and contradictions of his fictional characters. Nietzsche's impact was even more apparent. Malraux portrays the human will as an almost tangible dynamism driving his heroes into the very jaws of death. He establishes a dichotomy, however. The supreme individualist, the self-appointed *Übermensch*, destroys himself. Malraux's later protagonists suppress their singularity to discover the kinship and solidarity of a collective will to power.

Historian Oswald Spengler may also be counted among Malraux's formative influences in that he also provided a springboard for reaction, a theory to refute.

---

* In *André Malraux and the Tragic Imagination*, one of the soundest studies in English, W. H. Frohock develops a mythic interpretation of *shamanism*.

Among Malraux's diabolical fascinations, there is also the figure of Louis de Saint-Just, the handsome young daredevil of the French Revolution, ruthlessly cold-blooded in his pursuit of a spartan code of justice, and who ironically met death at age twenty-six, guillotined by fellow revolutionaries. His name haunts Malraux's pages as a symbol of the will to power.

The one contemporary who haunts Malraux is T.E. Lawrence—"Lawrence of Arabia." They are an astonishing twentieth-century example of Plutarchian "Parallel Lives." It was Lawrence's interest in archaeology that first drew him to the Arabian regions where he stayed on, from 1910 to 1918, joining the struggle for Arab unity against Turkish domination. Rising to the title of Colonel in the British Army, he also helped formulate foreign policy as an aide to Churchill after the war. Apart from their romantic biographies, there was a temperamental likeness between Lawrence and Malraux, both of whom sought glory of a kind, while maintaining an aura of mystery.

According to tradition, Lawrence was offered an "Arab kingship." Malraux wrote of "white chiefs" in *La Voie royale*, and continued to explore the "conqueror" theme throughout successive novels. It is uncertain whether Malraux had actually read Lawrence's *Seven Pillars of Wisdom*, which appeared in French translation in 1936, but the entire world knew the widely publicized Lawrence legend. Malraux indicates that he met Lawrence once "shortly before his death," which occurred on 13 May 1935, at the very moment when the newspaper *L'Intransigeant* was printing the last of Malraux's articles on his "discovery" of the kingdom of Sheba. Had that meeting inspired Malraux's flight over the Arab desert? Was he pursuing the "ghost" of Lawrence of Arabia—not knowing of course that T.E. Lawrence would soon be killed in a motorcycle accident?

One of Lawrence's alleged war experiences could not

have failed to fascinate Malraux. Captured by the Turks, he was stripped, brutally beaten, and raped by Turkish soldiers. In Lawrence's own account (which may be fact or fancy), he felt a "delicious warmth, probably sexual" sweep over him. Here was the conqueror conquered, the ultimate state of torture and humiliation feared by Malraux's early heroes, but with a psychological twist that neither Perken, Garine, nor Malraux himself, could possibly countenance.

Malraux never completed his projected study of Lawrence, tentatively titled *Le Démon de l'Absolu* (The Demon of the Absolute). In fact, each time he seemed to be coming to grips with aspects of the Lawrence legend, he failed to finish his project. *La Voie royale* was announced as the first volume of a series: *Les Puissances du désert* (Powers of the Desert); *Les Noyers de l'Altenburg* was to be part of a cycle called *La Lutte avec l'ange* (Battle with the Angel). His only recorded commentary, save from references in the *Antimémoires*, is a twelve-page article, published in 1946, in which Malraux interprets Lawrence as a prototype of his own heroes: a man who wanted to give meaning to his life by helping to change to order of the world.

What interests him most, however, is Lawrence's failure as a writer. According to Malraux, Lawrence was overcome with disappointment on reading the proofs of *The Seven Pillars*. He had hoped to achieve a work of "titanic" proportions, rivalling Dostoyevsky and Nietzsche, but on reading his own words in print, they seemed rather like the memoirs of a retired British officer. Malraux concludes that it is an error to rely too faithfully on chronological structure and the notes one jots down. The writer should strive for a "third dimension," a reconstruction of experience that transforms the mere chronicle of events into their mythic counterpart: not just "what happened" but the essence and the meaning. In this 1946 article, where he accuses Lawrence of having left his "portrait in the margin," Malraux was obviously wrestling with the notions of structure and style that would mark his own autoportrait, twenty years later, in the *Antimémoires.*

From his first book to his last, Malraux never ceased pursuing the demons that haunted him. The themes he pondered remained constant; the idea that "a man's image is to be found in the questions he asks" is one that recurs. But he was continually in search of new forms in which to frame his questions about conquest, identity, self-realization, the nature of fundamental man, the individual's relation to society—and, above all, the sense or senselessness of death.

When Malraux first started writing in the 1920s, French literature was dominated by a certain narcissism; the novel was largely static and introspective. There had been a vogue of war novels, of course, but with *Les Conquérants* in 1928, Malraux sounded a new voice as yet unheard in the twentieth century. Malraux took the novel out of its psychological "ivory tower" and plunged it into the machine-gun-ridden streets of Shanghai and Madrid. On the surface, his world of fiction was a world of violence, terror, and death. One British translator of *La Condition humaine* rather absurdly tried to capitalize on this by calling it *Storm in Shanghai.* The perceptive reader recognized that violence and upheaval were only the theatrical framework within which Malraux was dramatizing profound moral and metaphysical conflicts.

His call for a new definition of man, unfortunately, was answered by history before the European youth he was addressing could formulate a response. With the advent of fascism, they had no immediate choice in their destinies—except to choose sides. Malraux's intuitive vision of the twentieth century, before that vision became the stark reality of concentration camps, was a world in which men sought to constrain and dominate their fellow man, a world of torture and tanks, prison and death. In contemplating that nightmare universe, Malraux sought guidelines for survival or transcendence, and in so doing, set down the principles that would eventually be preempted by existentialism. Malraux's concept of an "absurd" universe meant that modern man could no longer rely on the outmoded absolute values of traditional western philosophy and religion. Man *is* what he chooses to become, defined by his acts. While these basic tenets were being further developed by Sartre and Camus, Malraux's thought adventured beyond to a more subtle concept: the operation of metamorphosis.

Starting with *Lunes en papier*, Malraux was obviously fascinated by change and transformation. In *L'Espoir*, Garcia states that the best thing a man can make of his life is "to transform the broadest possible range of experience into a heightened awareness of that experience." It is not just the events of our lives that count, but the way in which we let them modify our lives. Variations on the theme of metamorphosis continue to multiply as Malraux developed his theories on art and civilization. He believed that the key to self-knowledge and understanding was the transforming process, and that it also provided the key to fundamental man. The apple tree in *L'Espoir* and the walnut trees in *Les Noyers de l'Altenburg* are symbols of continuity through renewal: self-metamorphosis. The epigraph of the *Antimémoires* is that of an elephant contemplating his former lives; the book is Malraux's conscious effort to transform those various lives into a single life, his own, sub specie aeternitatis.

> "*Tel qu'en lui-même l'éternité le change . . .*"
> (Into himself eternity transforms him . . .)

This enigmatic verse (from Mallarmé's *tombeau* poem for Poe) suggests the process by which every artist spends his life creating himself within his work—which in turn becomes his monument after death. In Malraux's own terms, life is a succession of infinite possibilities; the choices that we make determine and define us. When death terminates that process, we become whole and final: the self that we have been creating, the scar we have left on the map.

Death, then, is the ultimate metamorphosis, transforming what *was* our life into a permanent, irremediable destiny. With death, the contradictions and the paradoxes are resolved; the man, one. Malraux was a private person who chose to spend his lifetime in the public arena, a dynamic man of action who reflected incessantly on art. His fascination with the east was a way of gaining a perspective on the west. His flirtation with Communism was an adventure in the self-discovery of his inherent nationalism, and his spiritual identification with De Gaulle showed a reversion to his innate hero-worship: the one demon he could not exorcise.

In composing his last "memorial" volumes, Malraux exercised the artist's option of self-metamorphosis, recording his paradoxical life not in oversimplified terms of true or false, fact or fiction—these are the shallow tools of the biographer—but by transforming his vast composite of experience into the "sur-reality" of metaphor and myth.

"What then is the relationship," he pondered in *Hôtes de Passage*, "between a man and the myth that he embodies?" Malraux had clearly saved the best question for last.

Bibliography

1. Major Works by André Malraux

La Tentation de l'Occident. Paris: Bernard Grasset, 1926.—*The Temptation of the West.* Translated by Robert Hollander. New York: Vintage Books, 1961.

Les Conquérants. Paris: Bernard Grasset, 1928.—*The Conquerors.* Translated by Winifred S. Whale. New York: Harcourt, Brace, 1929.

La Voie royale. Paris: Bernard Grasset, 1930.—*The Royal Way.* Translated by Stuart Gilbert. New York: Smith and Haas, 1935.

La Condition humaine. Paris: Gallimard, 1933.—*Man's Fate.* Translated by Haakon M. Chevalier. New York: Smith and Haas, 1934.

Le Temps du mépris. Paris: Gallimard, 1935.—*Days of Wrath.* Translated by Haakon M. Chevalier. New York: Random House, 1936.

L'Espoir. Paris: Gallimard, 1937.—*Man's Hope.* Translated by Stuart Gilbert and Alastair McDonald. New York: Random House, 1938.

Les Noyers de l'Altenburg. Lausanne: Editions du Haut-Pays, 1943.—*The Walnut Trees of Altenburg.* Translated by A. W. Fielding. London: John Lehmann, 1952.

La Psychologie de l'Art, 3 vols.: *Le Musée imaginaire, La Création Artistique, La Monnaie de l'absolu.* Geneva: Skira, 1947–50.—*The Psychology of Art (The Museum without Walls, The Artistic Act, The Twilight of the Absolute).* Translated by Stuart Gilbert. New York: Pantheon Books, 1949–51.

Saturne. Paris: Gallimard, 1950.—*Saturn: An Essay on Goya.* Translated by C. W. Chilton. New York and London: Phaidon, 1957.

Les Voix du silence. Paris: Gallimard, 1951.—*The Voices of Silence*. Translated by Stuart Gilbert. New York: Doubleday, 1953.

La Métamorphose des dieux. Paris: Gallimard, 1957.—The *Metamorphosis of the Gods.* Translated by Stuart Gilbert. New York: Doubleday, 1960.

Antimémoires. Paris: Gallimard, 1967.—*Anti-Memoirs*. Translated by Terence Kilmartin. New York: Holt, Reinhart and Winston, 1968.

Les Chênes qu'on abat. Paris: Gallimard, 1971—*Felled Oaks: Conversation with De Gaulle*. Translated by Irene Clephane. New York: Holt, Rinehart and Winston, 1972.

La Tête d'obsidienne. Paris: Gallimard, 1974.—*Picasso's Mask.* Translated by June Guicharnaud with Jacques Guicharnaud. New York: Holt, Rinehart and Winston, 1976.

Lazare. Paris: Gallimard, 1974.—*Lazarus*. Translated by Terence Kilmartin. New York: Holt, Reinhart and Winston, 1977.

Hôtes de Passage. (Transient Guests). Paris: Gallimard, 1975.

2. Books in English about André Malraux

Blend, Charles D. *André Malraux: Tragic Humanist.* Columbus: Ohio State University Press, 1963.

Blumenthal, Gerda. *André Malraux: The Conquest of Dread.* Baltimore: Johns Hopkins Press, 1960.

Frohock, W. M. *André Malraux and the Tragic Imagination.* Stanford: Stanford University Press, 1952.

Galante, Pierre. *Malraux*. New York: Cowles Book Company, 1971.

Gannon, Edward, S. J. *The Honor of Being a Man: The World of André Malraux.* Chicago: Loyola University Press, 1957.

Goldberger, Avriel. *Visions of a New Hero: The Heroic Life According to André Malraux and Earlier Advocates of Human Grandeur.* Paris: Lettres Modernes, 1965.

Greenlee, James W. *Malraux's Heroes and History.* De Kalb: Northern Illinois University Press, 1975.

Horvath, Violet M. *André Malraux: The Human Adventure.* New York: New York University Press, 1969.

Kline, Thomas Jefferson. *André Malraux and the Metamorphosis of Death.* New York and London: Columbia University Press, 1973.

Lacouture, Jean. *André Malraux.* New York: Pantheon Books, 1975.

Langlois, Walter G. *André Malraux: The Indochina Adventure.* New York: Praeger, 1966.

Payne, Robert. *A Portrait of André Malraux.* Englewood Cliffs: Prentice-Hall, Inc., 1970.

Righter, William. *The Rhetorical Hero: An Essay on the Aesthetics of André Malraux.* New York: Chilmark Press, 1964.

Wilkinson, David. *Malraux: An Essay in Political Criticism.* Cambridge: Harvard University Press, 1967.

3. Articles in English about André Malraux

Ball, Bertrand L., Jr. "Nature, Symbol of Death in *La Voie royale.*" *French Review,* XXV, No. 4 (February, 1962), pp. 390–95.

Baumgartner, Paul. "Solitude and Involvement: Two Aspects of Tragedy in Malraux's Novels." *French Review* XXXVIII, No. 6 (May, 1965), pp. 766–76.

Brée, Germaine (with Margaret Guiton). "André Malraux: Maker of Myths." In *An Age of Fiction: The French Novel from Gide to Camus.* New Brunswick: Rutgers University Press, 1957.

Brombert, Victor. "Malraux: Passion and Intellect." In *The Intellectual Hero: Studies in the French Novel.* Philadelphia: J. B. Lippincott, 1961.

Chevalier, Haakon M. "André Malraux: The Return of the Hero." *Kenyon Review,* II, No. 1 (Winter, 1940), pp. 35–46.

Chiaromonte, Nicola. "Malraux and the Demons of Action." *Partisan Review,* XV, Nos. 7 and 8 (July and August, 1948), pp. 776–89, and 912–23.

Flanner, Janet. "The Human Condition." In *Men and Monuments.* New York: Harper & Brothers, 1957.

Frank, Joseph. "Malraux's Image of Man." In *The Widening Gyre.* New Brunswick: Rutgers University Press, 1963.

Frohock, Wilbur M. "Malraux and the Poem of the Walnuts." In *Style and Temper: Studies in French Fiction 1925–1960.* Cambridge: Harvard University Press, 1967.

———— "Notes on Malraux's Symbols." *Romanic Review,* XLII, No. 4 (December, 1959), pp. 274–81.

Girard, René. "The Role of Eroticism in Malraux's Fiction." Yale French Studies, No. 11, pp. 49–54.

Herz, Micheline. "Woman's Fate." Yale French Studies, No. 18 (Winter, 1957), pp. 7–19.

Howe, Irving. "Malraux, Silone, Koestler." In *Politics and the Novel.* Cleveland and New York: Meridian Books, 1957.

Knight, Everett W. "Malraux." In *Literature Considered as Philosophy: The French Example.* London: Routledge and Kegan Paul, 1957.

Leefmans, Bert M-P. "Malraux and Tragedy: The Structure of *La Condition humaine.*" *Romanic Review,* XLIV, No. 3 (October 1953), pp. 208–14.

Magny, Claude-Edmonde. "Malraux the Fascinator." In *Malraux: A Collection of Critical Essays* (ed., R.W.B. Lewis). Englewood Cliffs: Prentice-Hall, Inc., 1964.

Peyre, Henri. "André Malraux." In *French Novelists Today.* New York: Oxford University Press, 1967.

Reck, Rima Drell. "André Malraux: Activist and Aesthete." In *Literature and Responsibility: The French Novelist in the Twentieth Century.* Baton Rouge: Louisiana State University Press, 1969.

Rees, G. O. "Animal Imagery in Novels of André Malraux." *French Studies,* IX, No. 2 (April, 1955), pp. 129–42.

Riffaterre, Michael. "Malraux's *Antimémoires*." Columbia Forum, XI, No. 4 (Winter, 1968), pp. 31–35.

Savage, Catherine. "Malraux and the Political Novel." In *Malraux, Sartre, and Aragon as Political Novelists*. Gainesville: University of Florida Press, 1964.

Sonnenfeld, Albert. "Malraux and the Tyranny of Time: The Circle and the Gesture." *Romanic Review*, LIV, No. 3 (October, 1963), pp. 198–212.

Stokes, Samuel E. "Malraux and Pascal." *Wisconsin Studies in Contemporary Literature*, VI, No. 3 (Autumn, 1965), pp. 286-92.

Trotsky, Leon. "The Strangled Revolution." In *Malraux: A Collection of Critical Essays* (ed., R.W.B. Lewis). Englewood Cliffs: Prentice-Hall, Inc., 1964.

Wilson, Edmund. "André Malraux." In *A Literary Chronicle: 1920–1950*. Garden City, N.Y.: Doubleday Anchor Books, 1956.

4. Collections of Articles in English about André Malraux

Malraux: Life and Work (ed., Martine de Courcel). New York and London: Harcourt, Brace, Jovanovich, 1976.

Malraux: A Collection of Critical Essays (ed., R. W. B. Lewis). Englewood Cliffs: Prentice-Hall, Inc., 1964.

Yale French Studies, No. 18 (Winter, 1957): "Passion and the Intellect, or André Malraux."

Index

MODERN LITERATURE MONOGRAPHS

In the same series (continued from page ii)

JOSÉ ORTEGA Y GASSET *Franz Niedermayer*
GEORGE ORWELL *Roberta Kalechofsky*
KATHERINE ANNE PORTER *John Edward Hardy*
EZRA POUND *Jeannette Lander*
MARCEL PROUST *James R. Hewitt*
RAINER MARIA RILKE *Arnold Bauer*
JEAN-PAUL SARTRE *Liselotte Richter*
UPTON SINCLAIR *Jon Yoder*
ISAAC BASHEVIS SINGER *Irving Malin*
KURT VONNEGUT *James Lundquist*
PETER WEISS *Otto F. Best*
EDITH WHARTON *Richard H. Lawson*
THORNTON WILDER *Hermann Stresau*
THOMAS WOLFE *Fritz Heinrich Ryssel*
VIRGINIA WOOLF *Manly Johnson*
RICHARD WRIGHT *David Bakish*
CARL ZUCKMAYER *Arnold Bauer*